The Sacred Garden of Lumbini
of Lumbini

Perceptions of Buddha's birthplace

Published in 2013 by the United Nations Educational,
Scientific and Cultural Organization
7, place de Fontenoy, 75352 Paris 07 SP, France

ISBN 978-92-3-001208-3

The designations employed and the presentation of material throughout this publication
do not imply the expression of any opinion whatsoever on the part of UNESCO
concerning the legal status of any country, territory, city or area or of its authorities, or
concerning the delimitation of its frontiers or boundaries.

The ideas and opinions expressed in this publication are those of the authors; they are
not necessarily those of UNESCO and do not commit the Organization.

For more information, contact
UNESCO Office in Kathmandu, Sanepa-2, Lalitpur, P.O. Box 14391, Kathmandu, Nepal
Tel: +977-1-555 4396 Fax: +977-1-555 4450
www.unesco.org/kathmandu
www.facebook.com/unescokathmandu

Compilation by Kai Weise

Based on contributions from Kosh Prasad Acharya, Basanta Bidari, Sayalay
Bhaddamanika, Roland Lin Chih-Hung, Anil Chitrakar, Robin Coningham, Christoph
Cüppers, Yukio Nishimura, Gyanin Rai, Herb Stovel and Kai Weise

Peer reviewed by Lisa Choegyal, Beena Poudyal and Sudarshan Raj Tiwari

Front cover photo: Sacred Garden, Lumbini, UNESCO/Nabha Basnyat Thapa
Back cover photo: Sacred Garden, Lumbini, Brenda Turnnidge
Graphic design: Kazi Studios, Nepal
Cover design: Kazi Studios, Nepal
Typeset: Kazi Studios, Nepal
Printed by: Hillside Printing Press

Printed in Kathmandu, Nepal

Contents

© Song Yan Gang

Foreword

A garden is ordered nature in the same way that religion is an ordered universe of values, beliefs and practices. Many religions have used the symbolic force of the garden as a peaceful locus amoenus, which embodies the mystical concept of paradise as the realm of the blessed.

Gardens surrounded the temples of the legendary land of Mesopotamia and Ancient Egypt. In the early development of India, China and Japan, sacred groves were part of the mythological landscapes. In contemporary times, they are still places of great reverence with their sacred trees similar to those that were popular in many early European countries.

Judeo-Christian mythology refers to sacred trees as the tree of knowledge of good and evil, and the tree of life. They are constituent elements of the Garden of Eden, the prototype of paradise.

In a similar vein, the gardens of the Qur'an, with their places to rest and contemplate, are the earthly equivalent of the life of paradise which is promised to believers.

Lumbini is one of these dreamlike, emblematic places.

Sacred trees, beautiful flowers, celestial splendor, eternal tranquility – these are the elements that constitute the place where Siddhartha, the Lord Buddha, was born. A modest grove in the Indus-Ganga Plain became the Sacred Garden of Lumbini.

This study is an attempt to describe in a multidimensional approach how this happened. It helps us better understand why this forest became a place of Outstanding Universal Value, which since millennia women and men visit 'with faith, curiosity and devotion' – as predicted by the Lord Buddha himself.

The many perspectives this study covers reflects the profound knowledge of the expert contributors to this unique project. We are indebted to all of them for their valued participation.

Without the generous support of representatives of the Oriental Cultural Heritage Sites Protection Alliance, we would not have been able to initiate this project. Our gratitude goes to them as well.

Axel Plathe
UNESCO Representative to Nepal

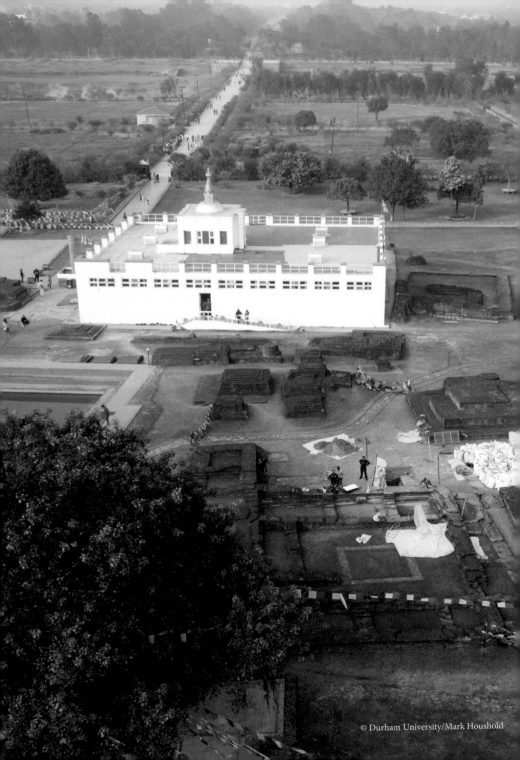

About the publication

This publication is based on the premise that Lumbini can be perceived from numerous viewpoints and that all viewpoints together facilitate the overall understanding of the birthplace of Lord Buddha. This perception sets the frame for the preparation of a management system, a mandatory requirement for a World Heritage Property.

At a meeting in Lumbini on 25 May 2010, Kai Weise, UNESCO consultant for the preparation of the Integrated Management Plan, presented to site managers and government authorities eight realms of understanding: in Buddhist texts; in historical texts; in archaeology; as part of the Kenzo Tange Master Plan; as a World Heritage Property; in an environmental context; and in association with the activities of visitors and pilgrims.

This eight-layer approach was the basis for the formulation of a UNESCO project funded by the Japanese Funds-in-Trust for the Preservation of the World Cultural Heritage that was aimed at supporting efforts to better manage Lumbini and address three other critical issues, namely broadening the knowledge based on Lumbini through archaeological research; ensuring the physical conservation of the vestiges in Lumbini; and preparing an improved lay-out of the Sacred Garden through a better understanding of the Kenzo Tange Master Plan.

A study was undertaken with funding from the Paris based non-governmental organization, Oriental Cultural Heritage Sites Protection Alliance, under the coordination of Kosh Prasad Acharya. The following experts were chosen for each of the eight perceptions: Christoph Cüppers for the chapter on Buddhist texts; Basanta Bidari for the chapter on historical texts; Robin Coningham for the chapter on archaeology; Yukio Nishimura for the chapter on Kenzo Tange Master Plan; Herb Stovel for the chapter on World Heritage; Anil Chitrakar for the chapter on environment; and Sayalay Bhaddamanika for the chapter on visitor activities.

Additionally, a study on visitors' expectations was carried out by Gyanin Rai. These studies became the basis for the preparation of the 'Guidelines for the physical planning of the Sacred Garden', a key component of the Integrated Management Framework for Lumbini, the Birthplace of Lord Buddha.

This publication presents the eight perceptions based on the experts' studies. It also incorporates additional information collected from various sources to provide a comprehensive and updated image of Lumbini. Lumbini is one of the most sacred places in the world.

Introduction

Lumbini is one of the most sacred places in the world. Over many centuries people have developed visions of the place where Gautama Buddha was born. There are certain attributes and characteristics that are part of the common understanding of Lumbini.

However, people have different perceptions, expectations and visions of Lumbini. They all are fragments of the overall picture of Lumbini. Bringing them all together provides a more comprehensive image of the sacred site.

A story narrated in a Buddhist scripture, Udana 68–69 nicely illustrates this phenomenon. Disciples asked Lord Buddha why the wandering hermits and scholars constantly argued about so many issues and never seemed to come to any consensus. Lord Buddha then related a tale about a king, who ordered for all the blind men in the ancient city of Śrāvastī to be gathered together in front of an elephant. Each was given a specific part of the elephant to touch. Each of them perceived a different aspect of the elephant and assumed the elephant to have only the features that they personally understood: the head is like a pot, the ear is like a winnowing basket, the tusk is like a share, the trunk is like a plough, the foot a pillar, the back a mortar, the tail a pestle and the tuft of the tail a brush. However, what they did not realize is that all these physical attributes put together make the elephant.

Then the Exalted One rendered this meaning by uttering this verse of uplift,

O how they cling and wrangle, some who claim
For preacher and monk the honoured name!
For, quarrelling, each to his view they cling.
Such folk see only one side of a thing.
(Udana, 68–69) (Buddha Dharma Education Association Inc. 2008)

Just like the blind men's quarrels, there have always been differences in perceptions about Lumbini, which is an entity just like the majestic elephant.

Siddhartha Gautama was born in the forest or garden near the village of Lumbini. There was a pool nearby where his mother Mayadevi bathed before giving birth. The religious texts give us varying descriptions of the birthplace of Lord Buddha.

> ... for when her time had nearly come, her father, King Suprabuddha Grihapati, sent the following message to King Suddhodana, at Kapilavastu: 'As I am informed that my daughter Maya, your Majesty's queen, is now with child, and already far advanced in pregnancy, and as I fear that when the child is born, my daughter will be short-lived, I have thought it right to ask you to permit my daughter to come back to me. I have prepared a palace in the Lumbini Garden for her reception' (Referring to the texts of the Lalita Vistara) (Lillie, 1883, p. 9).

> The biographical tradition was to locate the event of the Buddha's birth in the village (or Park) of Lumbini ... the park in question was named for her (Maya's mother) after having been made by Mayas's father, Suprabuddha, at a point half-way between the towns of Devdaha and Kapilvastu (Strong, 2001, p. 39).

> On the way, she and her party passed the pleasant Lumbini grove, where she stopped to enjoy the flowers and birdsong (Harvey, 2004, p. 16).

There has been some debate on whether the place near the village of Lumbini, where Siddhartha Gautama was born, was a forest or a garden. The discussion here revolves around the question whether the setting was a natural clearing in the forest or whether it was an artificially created environment.

> All of the Buddhist literature available agrees on the existence of a salvana ('sal forest'), a Lumbinivana ('Lumbini forest') and Mahavana ('great forest') in Kapilavastu. In these forests, the majority of trees were sal trees. The Buddhist literature also mentions that the Sakyas of Kapilavastu and Koliyas of Devadaha jointly maintained the garden of Lumbini. The garden

of Lumbini was also called Lumbinikanan, Lumbinivatika, Lumbiniupavana and Lumbinichittalatavana in earlier scriptures (Bidari, 2004, p. 65).

Most of what we know of historical Lumbini today derives from Buddhist literature, the accounts of visitors, and the facts provided by archaeological research. In 1896, when General Khadga Shamsher and archaeologist Anton Führer visited the site, Lumbini was in a state of total abandonment, and was almost completely covered by a series of mounds surrounded by

Nativity Sculpture

scattered ruins. Minor excavations were carried out, which were continued by Purna Chandra Mukherji in 1899.

However, the site did not go through any major physical changes until Kesher Shumsher J.B. Rana conducted his archaeological research at Lumbini between 1933 and 1939, which led to re-shaping the mound to expose some of the archaeological structures, building the Maya Devi Temple upon the plinth of the saptarathashikara, and enlarging the pond with successive terraces and a brick veneer (Rijal, 1979; Atzori et al., 2006).

An important part of knowledge about Lumbini is based on archaeological records. The archaeological research began with very crude methods and procedures, which improved immensely during the course of the nineteenth century. Today we do not have detailed reports on the earlier excavations that were carried out. The data from the more recent archaeological investigations provide us with a more precise understanding of the development of the site over the past two and a half millennia.

© Kai Weise

Praying in the Sacred Garden

During the second half of the nineteenth century, various structures were built around Lumbini such as the two monasteries, the rest houses and the Mahendra Pillar. When Japanese Architect Kenzo Tange prepared the Master Plan, which was completed in 1978, he envisioned the area around the main archaeological remains to be developed as a Sacred Garden with minimum infrastructure.

> All the modern structures existing in this area are to be removed, and only historically authenticated remains are to be restored (Tange and Utrec, 1978, p. 70).

The notions of tranquillity, universality and clarity that permeate the Kenzo Tange Master Plan reflect an attempt to translate the spirituality of the place into a physical environment.

> The terms pristine natural environment, sanctity, peace, harmony, etc. have been all used in the past, together with the various rituals performed by the pilgrims. As for the spiritual meaning, the definition of what specific tangible features best represent and embody it is less clear. However, a clear, shared vision of what sort of place would best convey the essence of Buddhist spirituality has not been defined. Again, this should be done based on a full understanding of the Outstanding Universal Value OUV of the site (Boccardi and Gupta, 2005, p. 3).

The 'Lumbini Institutions', a term which describes the international community living in Lumbini, have proposed that the Sacred Garden be declared a 'Five Precepts Zone', reflecting the basic Buddhist code of ethics. This notion was included in the Declaration of the Second World Buddhist Summit in 2004 (Declaration of the Second World Buddhist Summit, 2004).

However, in deciding on the creation of an appropriate and authentic environment for the Sacred Garden in the present day, there needs to be a clear understanding of the various changes of Lumbini's physical environment over the past century.

The numerous discussions since the inscription of Lumbini in the World Heritage List suggest that the physical plan for the Sacred Garden must ensure that an appropriate environment is created without having a negative impact on the archaeological remains. Beautification should not be carried out without a clear vision for the site.

> According to Kenzo Tange, the basic principle of design for the Sacred Garden is to create a quiet, natural environment by prohibiting the construction of new structures and by eliminating and relocating the existing structures (Atzori et al., 2006, p. 21).

The implementation of the grid of roads and drains that Kenzo Tange prescribes in his plan, has, however, impacted potential archaeological sites, which led to some voices calling for its amendment.

> … as far as the area of the World Heritage site is concerned, the Master Plan of Kenzo Tange should be reviewed and, if appropriate, amended (Boccardi and Gupta, 2005, p. 4).

Referring to the Kenzo Tange Master Plan, the Nomination Document submitted by Nepal to the World Heritage Committee in 1996 states that 'outside the nominated area but within the buffer zone, there are other religious buildings of the 20th century and buildings in use by the Lumbini Development Trust — all of which are scheduled for demolition' (ICOMOS, 1996). This call for demolition has been one of the major issues of contention, especially in respect to the two monasteries that exist in this area. Should it be decided that these are to be retained, clear conditions for their integration into the Sacred Garden need to be formulated.

Kenzo Tange determined the Sacred Garden as an area of one mile (1,600 metres) in the east-west direction and little less than one mile (1,360 metres) in the north-south direction around the main archaeological remains in Lumbini. By the construction of a water body and a levee to control the frequent floods in Lumbini, the area has been divided into two parts. Both were designed to encase and protect the main archaeological remains that constitute the most sacred elements of Lumbini. This segregation of the archaeological remains from the surrounding landscape constitutes a major intrusion into the existing landscape and was the main reason why only the inner Sacred Garden was inscribed as a World Heritage Property. As a consequence, the outer Sacred Garden, which the Kenzo Tange Master Plan defines as a 'wooded area' (Weise, 2008), has been neglected in past planning projects and discussions.

In the early days of civilization the relationship between humans and nature was very different from today's perceptions. The natural environment was often considered a place where all forms of mysterious beings lurked and one needed to protect oneself from them. However, nature brought humans close to the divinities. Furthermore, human beings were given plant-like qualities, for example during the Gupta period (second to sixth centuries CE).

Already in Bharhut and Sanchi the human figure is treated almost as a special kind of plant. In the art of Mathura, Sarnath, and various other centres of Gupta art, which thrived between the second and sixth centuries C.E., the human figure is separated from its mantle of plants and assumes the formal qualities of stalks and creepers (Lannoy, 1971, p. 24).

The close links of the human being with its natural environment, which are reflected above, is perceptible throughout the life of Siddhartha Gautama.

Today pilgrims and visitors come to Lumbini from all over the world to experience the place where Lord Buddha was born. They come to Lumbini to express their religious and spiritual sentiments in various ways, often linked to their diverse cultures. Some come to meditate, while others come to chant or beat on drums. Some come to offer gold leaves while others offer coins, incense or milk. They all come with the expectations of peace and harmony.

© Antoine Roulet

Mayadevi Temple

© Kai Weise

परिचय

लुम्बिनी विश्वका सर्वाधिक पावन स्थलहरूमध्येको एक हो । शताब्दीयौंदेखि मानिसहरूले गौ तम बुद्ध जन्मेको स्थानको विषयमा विभिन्न दृष्टिकोणहरू बनाएका छन् । लुम्बिनीसम्बन्धी मानिसहरूको साझा अवधारणाभित्र केही विशेषताहरू अन्तर्निहित छन् ।

लुम्बिनीको विषयमा मानिसहरूमा विभिन्न अवधारणा, अपेक्षा तथा दृष्टिकोणहरू रहेको पाइन्छ । ती सबै लुम्बिनीको समष्टिगत छविका अङ्गहरू हुन् जसलाई एकत्रित गर्दा यस पवित्र स्थलको अझ बृहत् छवि देखापर्छ ।

यस विशेषतालाई उदान ६८-६९ को कथाले राम्ररी दर्शाउछ । एकपटक शिष्यहरूले भगवान् बुद्धलाई सोधे कि किन घुमन्ते सन्यासी तथा भिक्षुहरू विविध विषयमा निरन्तर विवाद गरेर पनि कुनै सहमतिमा आउन सक्दैनन् । जवाफमा भगवान् बुद्धले एउटा राजाको कथा सुनाए । ती राजाले एक पटक प्राचीन नगर श्रवस्तीका सबै अन्धा मानिसहरूलाई एउटा हात्तीको अगाडि जम्मा हुने उर्दी जारी गरे । ती प्रत्येकलाई हात्तीको शरीरको स्पर्श गर्न लगाइयो । ती प्रत्येकले हात्तीको भिन्दाभिन्दै पक्षहरूको अनुभूति गरे र हात्तीमा आफूले जानेका कुराहरूकै जस्तो गुण रहे को अनुमान गरे - टाउको भाडाजस्तो, कान नाङ्लोजस्तो, दाह्रा फालीजस्तो, सुड हलोजस्तो, खुट्टा खम्बाजस्तो, ढाड मुसलीजस्तो, पुच्छर पन्यूजस्तो, पुच्छरका रौहरू बुरुशजस्तो । तथापि, यी सबै कुराहरूलाई मिलाउादा नै हात्ती बन्छ भन्ने कुराको अनुभूति भने तिनले गर्न सकेनन् ।

त्यसपछि प्रबुद्धले यस कुरालाई श्लोकद्वारा स्पष्ट पारे,
उपदेशक तथा सन्त भनी आडम्बर गर्नेहरू
कसरी अडिकन्छन् र विवाद गर्दछन् ।
आफ्नै धारणामा अडिकएर विवाद गर्नेहरू
कुनै कुराको एक मात्र पाटो देख्दछन् ।
(उदान, ६८-६९)

ती अन्धा मानिसहरूको मतभिन्नताजस्तै लुम्बिनीसम्बन्धी अवधारणाहरूमा भिन्नताहरू रहेको पाइन्छ जबकि लुम्बिनी हात्तीजस्तै विशाल कुरा हो ।

सिद्धार्थ गौतम लुम्बिनीको गाउनजिक रहेको उद्यानमा जन्मेका थिए । त्यहा नजिकै एउटा जलकुण्ड थियो जुनमा उनकी आमाले उनको जन्मभन्दा पहिले स्नान गरेकी थिइन् । धार्मिक आलेखहरूले भगवान् बुद्धको जन्मस्थलको फरक फरक विवरणहरू दिएका छन् ।

...जन्मको समय नजिकिदै गर्दा, उनका पिता राजा सुप्रबुद्ध गृहपतिले कपिलवस्तुका राजा शुद्धो धनलाई यस्तो सन्देश पठाए : 'मेरी छोरी, मौसुफकी महारानी माया गर्भवती भएकी र जन्मको समय निकट रहेको सन्देश प्राप्त भएको र जन्मपश्चात मेरी छोरी धेरै नबाच्ने मेरो शंका रहेको हुनाले मेरी छोरीलाई माइती पठाइबक्सनको लागि अनुरोध गर्नु उचित ठानो । उनको स्वागतार्थ मैले लुम्बिनीको उद्यानमा एउटा महल तयार गरिसकेको छु ।' (ललित विस्तारको आलेखबाट साभार) (लिल्ले, १८८३, पेज ९)

बुद्धको जन्मसम्बन्धी घटनालाई लुम्बिनीको गाउा (वा निकुञ्ज) साग लगेर जोड्ने बुद्ध जीवनीले खनको परम्परा रहिआएको छ ... यहा उल्लेखित निकुञ्जको नामाकरण मायावतीकी आमाको नामबाट गरिएको थियो जसलाई मायावतीका पिता राजा सुप्रबुद्धले देवदह र कपिलवस्तुको बीचमा पर्ने गरी निर्माण गर्न लगाएका थिए । (स्ट्रङ्ग, २००१, पेज ३९)

यात्राको क्रममा, उनी आफ्ना सङ्गीहरूसाग मनोहर लुम्बिनी वनमा आइपुगिन्, जहा उनी पुष्पलतिका तथा चराहरूको कलरव ध्वनिको आनन्द लिनको लागि रोकिइन् । (हार्भे, २००४, पेज १६)

लुम्बिनी ग्राम नजिकै सिद्धार्थ गौतम जन्मिएको ठाउा कुनै वन थियो वा उद्यान थियो भन्ने विषयमा विवाद रहेको छ । यस विषयको छलफल उक्त परिवेश वनभित्र प्राकृतिक रुपमै रहेको खुला स्थान थियो वा कुनै मानव निर्मित वातावरण थियो भन्ने कुराको वरिपरि केन्द्रित रहेको छ ।

सबै उपलब्ध बौद्ध ग्रन्थहरूले कपिलवस्तुमा सालवन (सालको वन), लुम्बिनी वन (लुम्बिनीको वन) तथा महावन (ठूलो वन) को अवस्थितिलाई स्वीकार गर्छन् । यी वनहरूमा अधिकांश रुखहरू साल प्रजातिका थिए । कपिलवस्तुका शाक्यहरू तथा देवदहका कोलियहरू दुबैले संयुक्त रुपमा लुम्बिनी उद्यानको हेरचाह गर्दथे भनेर पनि बौद्ध ग्रन्थले उल्लेख गरेको छ । त्यसअधिका ग्रन्थहरूमा लुम्बिनी उद्यानलाई लुम्बिनीकानन, लुम्बिनीबाटिका, लुम्बिनीउपवन तथा लुम्बिनीचित्तलतावन भनेर पनि उल्लेख गरेको पाइन्छ । (बिडारी, २००४, पेज ६५)

© Kai Weise

Close up of Nativity Statue taken in 2011

लुम्बिनीको ऐतिहासिकताको विषयमा आज हामीलाई ज्ञान भएका अधिकांश कुराहरू बौद्ध ग्रन्थ, यात्रीहरूका विवरण, तथा पुरातात्त्विक अन्वेषणका तथ्यहरूबाट प्राप्त भएका हुन् । सन् १८९६ मा जर्नेल खड्ग शमशेर र पुरातत्त्वविद् एन्टोन फुहरर यस स्थलमा आउादा लुम्बिनी भग्नावशेषहरूले घेरिएको र थुम्काथुम्कीहरूले भरिएको परित्यक्त स्थलको रुपमा रहेको थियो । त्यहा सामान्य उत्खनन्कार्यहरू गरिए जसलाई पछि सन् १८९९ मा पूर्णचन्द्र मुखर्जीले निरन्तरता दिए ।

सन् १९३३ देखि १९३९ का बीचमा लुम्बिनीमा केशर शमशेर जबरले आफ्नो पुरातात्त्विक अन्वेषण नगरेसम्म उक्त स्थलमा कुनै विशेष भौतिक परिवर्तनहरू भएनन् । त्यस अन्वेषणपश्चात नै केही पुरातात्त्विक अवशेषहरू अनावृत हुने गरी त्यहाको थुम्काको आकारमा परिवर्तन गर्ने, सप्तरथशिखरको जगमाथि मायादेवी मन्दिरको निर्माण गर्ने र क्रमिक खुड्किलाहरू र झाटाको तहहरूसमेत समावेश गरी त्यहाको जलकुण्डको आकारमा वृद्धि गर्ने कामहरू भए । (रिजाल, १९७९, यूनेस्को, २००६)

लुम्बिनीसम्बन्धी ज्ञानको महत्त्वपूर्ण अंश पुरातात्त्विक अभिलेखहरूमा आधारित छन् । त्यहा भएका प्रारम्भिक पुरातात्त्विक अन्वेषणहरू अवैज्ञानिक विधि र प्रक्रियाबाट शुरु गरिए जुन उन्नाइसौं शताब्दीसम्म आइपुग्दा धेरै परिष्कृत भए । आज हामीसाग विगत उत्खननहरूको विस्तृत प्रतिवेदनहरू छैन । पछिल्ला पुरातात्त्विक अन्वेषणहरूको तथ्याङ्कले गत अढाइ हजार वर्षको अवधिमा उक्त स्थलको विकास कसरी भएको हुनुपर्छ भन्ने विषयमा यथार्थ विवरण दिन्छ ।

उन्नाइसौं शताब्दीको उत्तरार्द्धतिर लुम्बिनीको वरिपरि दुइटा बिहारहरू, धर्मशाला तथा महेन्द्र स्तम्भजस्ता विभिन्न संरचनाहरूको निर्माण भयो । जापानी वास्तुकार केन्जो टाङ्गेले लुम्बिनीको गुरुयोजना (जुन सन् १९७८ मा तयार भयो) बनाउादा उनले मुख्य पुरातात्त्विक अवशेषहरू वरिपरिको क्षेत्रमा न्यूनतम पूर्वाधारहरू रहने गरी पवित्र उद्यानको रुपमा विकास गर्ने परिकल्पना गरे ।

यस क्षेत्रमा रहेका सबै आधुनिक संरचनाहरू हटाइनुपर्छ र ऐतिहासिक रुपमा प्रमाणीकृत अवशेषहरूलाई मात्र रहन दिइनुपर्छ । (टाङ्गे, १९७८, पेज ७०)

केन्जो टाङ्गेको गुरुयोजनामा निहित शान्त वातावरण, विश्वव्यापी महत्त्व र स्पष्टताका अवधारणाहरूले उक्त स्थानको आध्यात्मिकतालाई भौतिक वातावरणमा परिणत गर्ने प्रयासलाई प्रतिबिम्बित गर्दछन् ।

विशुद्ध प्राकृतिक वातावरण, पवित्रता, शान्ति, सौहार्दताजस्ता शब्दावलीहरू विगतमा तीर्थालुहरूले गर्ने विभिन्न अनुष्ठानहरूसागसागै प्रयोग गरिन्थ्यो । आध्यात्मिकताको प्रश्नमा कुन चाहि निश्चित मूर्त कुराले यसलाई राम्ररी दर्शाउाछ र त्यसमा यो अन्तर्निहित हुन्छ भन्ने कुरा स्पष्ट छैन । तथापि कुन चाहि स्थानले बौद्ध आध्यात्मिकताको सारलाई अझ राम्ररी दर्शाउाछ भन्ने कुराको स्पष्ट र साझा दृष्टिकोण परिभाषित गरिएको छैन । फेरि पनि, यस कुरालाई उक्त स्थलको अनुपम विश्वव्यापी महत्त्वको समष्टिगत बुझाइको आधारमा तय गरिनुपर्छ । (बोकार्डी २००५, पेज ३)

लुम्बिनी संघ (लुम्बिनीमा बसोवास गर्ने अन्तर्राष्ट्रिय समुदायलाई बुझाउने शब्द) ले मूलभूत बौद्ध आचार संहिता प्रतिबिम्बित हुने गरी पवित्र उद्यानलाई 'पञ्च शील क्षेत्र' घोषित गर्नुपर्ने

प्रस्ताव गरेको छ । यस अवधारणालाई सन् २००४ को दोश्रो बौद्ध सम्मेलनको घोषणापत्रमा समावेश गरिएको थियो ।

तथापि, आजको दिनमा पवित्र उद्यानको लागि उपयुक्त र प्रामाणिक वातावरण के हुन सक्छ भन्ने कुरा तय गर्दा विगतका शताब्दीहरूमा लुम्बिनीको भौतिक वातावरणमा भएका विभिन्न परिवर्तनहरूलाई स्पष्टसग बुझ्नु जरुरी हुन सक्छ ।

लुम्बिनीलाई विश्व सम्पदा सूचीमा सूचीकृत गरेपछि भएका असंख्य छलफलहरूले त्यहा गरिने वातावरणको विकासले त्यहाका पुरातात्त्विक अवशेषहरूमा नकारात्मक असर पार्न नहुने कुरा सुनिश्चित गरिनुपर्छ भन्ने देखाएका छन् । सौन्दर्यवर्धन कार्यहरू उक्त स्थलको स्पष्ट दृष्टिकोण नबनाइकन गरिनु हुदैन ।

केन्जो टाङ्गेको भनाइअनुसार, पवित्र उद्यानको डिजाइनको मूलभूत सिद्धान्त नयाँ निर्माण कार्यहरूलाई प्रतिबन्धित गरेर र विद्यमान् संरचनाहरूलाई हटाएर एवं स्थानान्तरण गरेर शान्त, प्राकृतिक वातावरणको सृजना गर्नु नै हो । (युनेस्को, २००६, पेज २१)

केन्जो टाङ्गेले आफ्नो योजनामा प्रस्ताव गरेको बाटो र ढलहरूको कार्य गर्दा यसले संभावित पुरातात्त्विक स्थलहरूलाई असर पुर्‍याउन सक्ने देखिएको छ जसले गर्दा गुरुयोजनालाई संशोधन गर्नुपर्ने विषयमा केही आवाजहरू उठिरहेका छन् ।

... जहासम्म विश्व सम्पदा स्थलको प्रश्न छ, केन्जो टाङ्गेको गुरुयोजनालाई पुनरावलोकन गरी यथोचित संशोधन गरिनुपर्छ । (बोकार्डी, २००५, पेज ४)

केन्जो टाङ्गेको गुरुयोजनालाई उद्धृत गर्दै सन् १९९६ मा नेपालले विश्व सम्पदा समितिलाई बुझाएको दस्तावेजले 'मनोनित क्षेत्रभन्दा बाहिर तर सन्निकट क्षेत्रभन्दा भित्र रहेका २०औं शताब्दीका केही धार्मिक भवनहरू र लुम्बिनी विकास कोषले प्रयोग गर्दै आएको केही भवनहरू सबै भत्काइने' भनी स्पष्टसग उल्लेख छ (इकोमस, १९९६) । खासगरी यस क्षेत्रमा रहेका दुई बिहारहरूको विषयलाई लिएर भवन भत्काउने कुरा विवादमा पर्दै आएको छ । यदि तिनलाई नभत्काइने हो भने पवित्र उद्यानमा तिनलाई आबद्ध गराउने स्पष्ट शर्तहरू तय गरिनुपर्छ ।

केन्जो टाङ्गेले लुम्बिनीमा रहेका पुरातात्त्विक अवशेष वरिपरि पूर्व-पश्चिम दिशामा एक माइल (१६०० मीटर) र उत्तर-दक्षिण दिशामा एक माइलभन्दा अलि कम (१३६० मीटर) कायम गरी पवित्र उद्यानको क्षेत्रनिर्धारण गरे । लुम्बिनीमा साधै आइरहने बाढीको नियन्त्रण गर्नको लागि जलकुण्ड र जलबन्धको निर्माणले उक्त क्षेत्रलाई दुई भागमा विभक्त गरेको छ । यी दुवै कुरहरूको डिजाइन लुम्बिनीको सर्वाधिक पवित्र तत्त्व निहित रहेको प्रमुख पुरातात्त्विक अवशेषहरूलाई आवरण प्रदान गरी सुरक्षित राख्नको लागि गरिएको थियो । लुम्बिनीको क्षेत्रमा पुरातात्त्विक अवशेषहरूलाई वरिपरिको भूभागबाट छुट्ट्याइनु सो क्षेत्रको भूपरिदृश्यमा गरिएको मुख्य हस्तक्षेप थियो जसले गर्दा पवित्र उद्यानलाई मात्र विश्व सम्पदाको रुपमा सूचीकृत गरियो । परिणामस्वरुप केन्जो टाङ्गेको गुरुयोजनाले 'वन क्षेत्र' (वाइजे, २००८) भनी परिभाषित गरेको पवित्र उद्यानभन्दा बाहिरको क्षेत्र विगतका कार्यक्रम तथा छलफलमा ओझेलमा पर्न गयो ।

Detail of inscription on Ashoka Pillar taken in 2013

सभ्यताका प्रारम्भिक दिनहरूमा मानव र प्रकृतिवीचको सम्बन्ध वर्तमान दृष्टिले विल्कुलै भिन्न थियो । प्रायः प्राकृतिक वातावरणलाई सारा रहस्यमय जीव लुक्ने ठाउँको रुपमा हेरिन्थ्यो र आफूलाई तिनीहरूबाट सुरक्षित राख्नुपर्ने हुन्थ्यो । तथापि, प्रकृतिले मानवलाई देवत्वको नजिक पुऱ्यायो । त्यसबाहेक, मानवहरूलाई वानस्पतिक गुणहरू पनि दियो, जस्तै गुप्त कालमा (इसाकालको दोश्रोदेखि छैठौं शताब्दीसम्म)

वरहुट र साँचीमा मानव शरीरलाई विशेष प्रकारको विरुवाको रुपमा हेर्न थालिसकिएको थियो । मथुरा, सारनाथका कलाकौशलमा र इसाकालको दोश्रोदेखि छैठौं शताब्दीसम्म रहेको गुप्त कलाका अन्य विभिन्न केन्द्रहरूमा मानव शरीरलाई यसको वानस्पतिक आवरणबाट हटाई डाठ र लताहरूको गुणयुक्त स्वरुपमा हेरिन थालिएको थियो । (लनोय, १९७१, पेज २४)

माथि दर्शाइएको मानव र प्रकृतिवीचको निकट सम्बन्ध सिद्धार्थ गौतमको जीवनकालभरि अनुभूत गर्न सकिन्छ ।

आज संसारभरिका तीर्थालु तथा पर्यटकहरू भगवान् बुद्ध जन्मेको स्थानको अनुभूति लिन लुम्बिनी आउछन् । तिनीहरू आफ्ना धार्मिक तथा आध्यात्मिक भावनाहरूलाई प्रायः आफ्ना विविध संस्कृतिसाग गाँसिएका विभिन्न तरिकाहरूबाट अभिव्यक्त गर्न लुम्बिनी आउछन् । कोही ध्यान गर्न आउछन् भने कोही मन्त्रोच्चारण गर्न आउछन् । कोही सुनको मोलम्वा चढाउन आउछन् भने कसैले भेटी रुपैयाँ, धूप वा दूध चढाउछन् । ती सबै शान्ति र सौहार्दताको कामना लिएर आउछन् ।

(Nepali version of introduction)

© Brenda Turnnidge

Perception One

The garden of the gods. Lumbini in early Buddhist literature

The Buddhist texts were first written in Pali in the first century BCE and others followed in Sanskrit and Tibetan and in Chinese translations. Through the centuries, further commentaries and embellishments were added. In various texts compiled throughout the long history of Buddhism, Lumbini is described, interpreted and projected. These texts give a sense of what Lumbini is considered to be from the Buddhist perspective.

Content

Interpretation of Buddhist literature. In search for historic evidence. An overview of Buddhist texts. The biographies of the many Buddhas. The creation and transmission of Buddhist literature. Lumbini, where I was born.

References

This chapter is based on contributions by Christoph Cüppers.

Interpretation of Buddhist literature

Anecdotes about the life of Lord Buddha are very old and as numerous as Buddhist traditions themselves. From the South-Asian records, we know that the biography of Lord Buddha was constantly developed following his physical death, his *parinirvāna*. As so often in the case of founders of religions, contemporaneous material would have been sufficient for the first few generations, who still may have preserved some direct memory of the great master. The communities of followers that came later require a complete and more or less well-organized vita of their venerated founder. As a rule, the more distant the historical present is from the founder's (alleged) lifetime, the more the need for a fully developed biography arises.

After textual narratives, the stories are usually transferred into other media of human cultural expression such as pictorial depiction. We have clear evidence from Buddhist literature, but also from modern anthropological material of festivities and connected rituals performed on the occasion of the birth of the Buddha.

The problems, with which scholars are confronted when reading these texts as historical sources has been emphasized by Harry Falk quoting the French scholar André Bareau:

> Bareau has gone to great lengths to show that authoritative Buddhist texts, in expatiating upon the birthplace of the Buddha, are highly contradicting in the details, as if the authors had never personally been to the scene of the event. The place is called a 'village' (gāma) by Asoka; according to the Suttanipāta 683, the birth village (gāma) of the Buddha is located in the country (janapada) belonging to Lumbinī; in the Nidānakathā, Lumbinī is only a forest ... Chinese translations speak in terms of a 'garden' or 'park' ... The tree under which the Buddha was born is called in the sources either lumba ... or pippala ... shāla ... plaksa ... or else, in travel guides Asoka ... There is, therefore, every justification for Bareau's warning not to exaggerate the authority of the written sources in their details.
>
> If we seek statements that offer a balanced account of the site as it actually was, we are forced to resort to the travel reports of foreigners, namely those written by Chinese and Tibetans (Falk, 1998, p. 3).

In search for historic evidence

There was a fully developed tradition on the last days of the 'Awakened One', the *Mahāparinibbānasuttānta* in the Pāli canon of the *Theravādin*, which finds its parallel in the Sanskrit version of the Sārvāstivādin and at different places in other Buddhist works. Some scholars have argued that this is the only piece of Buddhist canonical literature, which breathes the spirit of Lord Buddha himself.

The realistic overtones and contents of these texts have attracted scholars and have certainly contributed to historical research on the life of Lord Buddha, a culmination point of which is the publication of the well-known and impressive proceedings of a conference on the dating of Lord Buddha in Göttingen, edited by Heinz Bechert (Bechert, 1991; Bechert, 1992). The impressive range of articles collected in these three volumes could, however, not solve the problem of the historical dating completely, but in tracing traditions on Lord Buddha's last days and his *parinirvāna*, this publication did indeed reveal the rich variety and diversity of the different Buddhist traditions even in case of their most common subject – the life of their founder.

It is no wonder that this part of Lord Buddha's life has attracted the attention of Western Buddhist scholars, who from the very beginning of the discovery of Buddhism as a religion, had become virtually obsessed with the idea and the possibility of retrieving historical facts from this very religious tradition (Allen, 2002; Allen, 2008).

© Kai Weise

The outcome of this approach, which definitely was embedded in a colonial context and discourse, was that different aspects of the textual, art-historical and archaeological sources became neglected during the hunt for positivist results, which tried to answer questions like: did it, and if so, when, where and how did it happen?

The most excessive use of almost only one strand of textual sources, the Pāli-tradition in its canonical and late commentarial textual representation, was completed by Schumann in 1989. Against this historicist undertaking stands the biographical sketch by Strong 2001. As has already been pointed out by other scholars, the fact that Buddhism was an extinct religion on the sub-continent opened up the possibility to reconstruct a Buddhist past without the interference of a modern continuation and tradition as in the case of Hinduism.

Major divisions of the Tripitaka

Vinaya-pitaka **'Basket of Discipline'**	*Abhidhamma-pitaka* **'Basket of Higher Teachings'**	*Sutta-pitaka* **'Basket of Discourses'**
Suttavibhanga Mahavibhanga Bhikkhunivibhanga Khandhaka Mahavagga Cullavagga Parivara	Dhammasangani Vibhanga Dhatukatha Puggalapaññatti Kathavatthu Yamaka Patthana	Digha Nikaya Majjhima Nikaya Samyutta Nikaya Anguttara Nikaya Khuddaka Nikaya Khuddakapatha Dhammapada Udana Itivuttaka Sutta Nipata Vimanavatthu Petavatthu Theragatha Therigatha Jataka Niddesa Patisambhidamagga Apadana Buddhavamsa Cariyapitaka Nettippakarana Petakopadesa Milindapañha

Source: (Buddha Dharma Education Association Inc. 2008)

An overview of Buddhist texts

There are a vast number of Buddhist scriptures; however there is not a single text that is considered authoritative by all schools of Buddhism. Each school of Buddhism has its own set of texts, which it considers important. The scriptures are understood to be the teachings of the historic Buddha, which was initially passed on orally from numerous generations until it was written down under various circumstances. Variations and different interpretations crept into the transmissions of these teachings early in the history of Buddhism. Later scriptures also include the teachings of other enlightened masters. These scriptures provide directions on how to understand and practice to gain self-enlightenment.

Buddhist scripture can be categorized into three types:

The *Vinaya* are texts that record the rules of the monastic order for nuns and monks. The *Vinaya* includes the rules governing the life of every Theravada monk or nun along with the way they live in a harmonous relationship amongst one another and with their lay supports, upon whom they depend for all their material needs.

The *Abhidharma* (Sanskrit) or *Abhidhamma* (Pali) are texts of philosophical discourse that provide analysis of the *sūtras*. *Abhidharma* literally means higher doctrine or phenomena. It provides the theoretical framework to the Buddhist path to enlightentment.

The *Sūtras* (Sanskrit) or *Sutta* (Pali), which means thread, are texts which are generally considered to contain the sermon of the historic Buddha or one of his major disciples. *Sūtras* come in different lengths from several lines to entire books.

Buddhist scriptures are broadly divided into Theravāda and Mahāyāna canons. Theravādins do not consider the Mahayana scriptures to be authentic. Though Mahāyāna Buddhists do consider the Theravāda canon to be authentic, in some cases they consider their own scriptures to have superseded the Theravāda canons. However, within Mahāyāna Buddhism there exist different viewpoints concerning the importance of various scriptures.

The scriptures of the Theravāda school are collected in the *Tipitaka* (Pali) or *Tripitaka* (Sanskrit) meaning the three baskets. These are the *Vinaya-pitaka* or the Basket of Discipline, the *Abhidhamma-pitaka* (*Abhidharma-pitaka* in Sanskrit) or the Basket of Higher Teaching and the *Sutta-pitaka* (*Sutra-pitaka* in Sanskrit) or the Basket of Discourses. The most complete and common version of the *Tripitaka* is in the Pali language, also called the Pali Canon. The Pali Canon is thought to be the words of the historical Buddha and some of his disciples, preserved it for a time by oral tradition and it was then written down in the first century BCE. Some *sutras* in Sanskrit exist that correspond to the Pali Canons of early discourses and are called the Agamas. Different versions of the *Abhidharma* also exist in fragments, the most intact coming from the Saravastivada sect that emerged in the third century BCE (O'Brien).

The Mahāyāna sutras are said to have been written by unknown authors between the first century BCE and the fifth century CE and a few even later than that. Though some are linked to the sermons of the historic Buddha, most consider them to be later interpretations with deep wisdom and spiritual value, therefore revered as *sutras*. The original Mahāyāna sutras are considered to have been written in Sanskrit. These original texts are lost and the oldest existing versions are the Chinese translations. Some scholars suggest that the texts in Chinese are the actual original versions, with the claim that they were translated from Sanskrit to give them their authenticity.

The Mahāyāna *sutras* often consist of many independent *sutras*. The Avatamsaka Sūtra (Flower Ornament Sūtra) consists of large important, independent *sutras*, and these records the higher teachings of Lord Buddha to Bodhisattvas and other spiritual beings. The Brahmajala Sūtra (Brahma's Net Sūtra) contains the Ten Major Precepts of Mahāyāna followers, and the Bodhisattva Precepts. The Prajnaparamita Sūtras (perfection of wisdom) consists of 40 sūtras including the Vajracchedika Prajnaparamita Sūtra (Diamond Sūtra) which sets forth the doctrines of Sunyata (emptiness) and Prajna (wisdom). The Prajnaparamita-Hrdaya Sūtra (Heart Sūtra) is one of the smallest but very popular *sutras*, which has an emphasis on emptiness. The Vaipulya group of forty-nine independent *sutras* includes one of the oldest *sutras* the Ratnakuta Sūtra (Jewel Heap Sutra). Here the philosophy of the middle is developed, which later becomes the basis for the Madhyamaka teaching of Najarjuna. The Saddharma Pundarika Sūtra (Lotus Sūtra) teaches the identification of the historical Buddha, with the Transcendental Buddha. There are three sutras that form the doctrinal basis of the Pureland School: the Amitabha Sūtra (Shorter Amitabha Sūtra), the Amitayurdyhana Sūtra (Meditation Sūtra) and Longer Amitabha Sūtra. These describe the Blessings and Virtues of Amitabha Buddha and his Pureland, and discusses rebirth (Buddha Dharma Education Association Inc. 2008).

Public domain

Heart Sūtra, Buddhist text from Hōryū-ji in Nara, Japan

The biographies of the many Buddhas

From the last episode in the life of Lord Buddha, so lively described in the *Mahāparinirvānasūtra*, three other episodic complexes have been elaborated on and legitimized, which are mentioned in this very text in form of the four main places of pilgrimage: the 'skeleton' of the Buddha biography seems to have consisted of the four major events — birth, enlightenment, first sermon and *parinirvāna* (Waldschmidt, 1950, 1951, pp. 388 –390). Here we already grasp a first step of another way of dealing with the biography of Lord Buddha — and it is no wonder that it did not attract the interest of Western scholars in the same way: a stereotyped string of important events, which were rather measured by their stereological value and function than by a strict sense of 'realism'.

The very concept underlying the quotation from the *Mahāparinirvānasūtra* eventually led to the second biographical concept in the early Buddhism tradition: the idea that all Buddhas – the historical one, the uncountable past ones, and the future one – have virtually the same biographical framework. Only the names of persons, important items (such as the *bodhi*-tree) and places were different in every Buddha-vita and thus individualized the topic hagiographical scheme. This is well reflected in the Pāli Apadānasuttānta and the Sanskrit Avadānasūtra, in which the life of the Buddha Vipaśyin (Pāli Vipassī) is related by the Buddha Śākyamuni himself (Waldschmidt, 1953, 1956, and Fukita, 2003. On Buddha-vitae in the Theravāda tradition, see Reynolds, 1976, 1997, and Woodward, 1997).

The idea of Buddhas of the past – and in consequence also the Buddha of the future, Maitreya – having led similar lives as the Gautama Śākyamuni Buddha seems to project these Buddhas and with them, the historical Buddha into a mythical, almost timeless and space less sphere. This very idea or belief in Buddhas of the past is revealed to be very early through the Ashokan Nigālī Sāgar inscription. This shows that in the early period, the idea of the Buddhas of the past was still very much a concrete, tangible and accessible reality, which could be visited on a pilgrimage tour. The Chinese pilgrims, Faxian and Xuanzang, report on the *stūpas* of the Buddhas Krakucchanda and Kanakamuni near Kapilavastu, although it is not clear to what extent these places were still frequented places of veneration (Deeg, 2003, pp. 36 – 43; Deeg, 2005, pp. 324 – 327).

The creation and transmission of Buddhist literature

Buddhist literature begins with the oral instruction given by Lord Buddha to his immediate disciples. It is however not known in what language he made his discourses. It is assumed that the language used at the time was not Vedic Sanskrit, but a vernacular such as the eastern middle Indo-aryan language, Māgadhī (Hinüber, 1997, p. 4).

The *Theravādin*s assume that their canon has come down in the language used by Lord Buddha, which they consequently call Māgadhī as well as Pāli.

However, it has been understood that the Theravāda canon is much later than Lord Buddha and that Pāli never was a spoken language. Pāli might have been a lingua franca with roots in a language spoken in western India but derived from an earlier eastern version (Hinüber 1986, pp. 37-40, 71). No original text of the very beginnings of Buddhism has come to us. Therefore, it is evident that the texts as found in the Theravāda canon, though the oldest Buddhist texts surviving, are the result of a lengthy and complicated development.

All editions of the Buddhist Canon are ultimately based on palm leaf manuscripts handed down in the Theravāda countries. The continuous manuscript tradition with complete texts begins only during the late 15th century. There are earlier fragments of texts found engraved in stone and on gold or silver folios. The oldest fragment of Theravāda *Vinaya*, copied during the eighth or ninth century, was found in Kathmandu. So the available texts of Theravāda literature were written down some 2,000 years after Lord Buddha.

For more than one, if not two, centuries the texts were and had to be handed down orally, as there was no script in India (Hinüber, 1989). Consequently, the texts were in constant danger of being changed or tampered with by individual monks such as Purāna, who came too late to attend the first council and refused to accept the received version of the texts, but preferred to stick to the wording as he had heard it personally from Lord Buddha. This is the first hint at a split of text tradition.

To guard the texts against alterations, Buddhists developed some means to check their authenticity at a very early date. These are the four *mahāpadesas* 'the great arguments': a text should have been heard (1) directly from the Buddha; (2) from a knowledgeable community of monks; (3) from learned Theras, or; (4) from a single competent Thera. Then it needs to be verified as to whether or not the content concurs with *Vinaya* and Suttantas. This at the same time presupposes some collection, against which to check it, some kind of nucleus from which a canon developed.

© Kai Weise

Gold leaf offerings on archaeological remains of a stupa

The Nativity Story: Translations of texts

The following pages provide a series of examples of texts from various sources that refer to Lumbini and the nativity story. The texts are translations from both Pāli and Sanskrit sources which provide us with an overall impression of the Buddhist image of Lumbini during the birth of Gautama Buddha.

Mahāpadāna-sutta (Dīgha-nikāya 14)

It is the rule that whereas other women give birth sitting or lying down, it is not so with the Bodhisattva's mother, who gives birth standing up. That is the rule (Dhammatā: that which is in accordance with Dhamma as universal law).

It is the rule that when the Bodhisattva issues from his mother's womb, devas welcome him first, and then humans. That is the rule.

It is the rule that when the Bodhisattva issues from his mother's womb he does not touch the earth. Four devas receive him and place him before his mother, saying: 'Rejoice, Your Majesty, a mighty son has been born to you!' That is the rule.

It is the rule that when the Bodhisattva issues from his mother's womb, he issues forth stainless, not defiled by water, mucus, blood or any impurity, pure and spotless. Just as when a jewel is laid on muslin from Kāsī, the jewel does not stain the muslin, or muslin the jewel. Why not? Because of the purity of both. In the same way, the Bodhisattva issues forth stainless ... That is the rule (Walshe, 1998, p. 204, 1.24-1.27).

Acchariyabbhutadhamma-sutta (Majjhima-nikāya 123)

Other women give birth seated or lying down, but not the Bodhisattva's mother. The Bodhisattva's mother gave birth to him standing up.

When the Bodhisattva came forth from his mother's womb, first devas received him, then human beings.

When the Bodhisattva came forth from his mother's womb, he did not touch the earth. The four young gods received him and set him before his mother, saying: 'Rejoice, O Queen, a son of great power has been born to you.'

When the Bodhisattva came forth from his mother's womb, he came forth unsullied, unsmeared by water or blood or any kind of impurity – clean, and unsullied. Suppose a gem is placed on a Kāśī cloth, then the gem would neither smear the cloth nor the cloth the gem. Why is that? Because of the purity of both (Nanamoli, 1972, p. 982).

Sanskrit Buddhacarita, Canto I, 8 ff

In that glorious grove the queen ... proceeded to a couch overspread with an awning. Then ... from the side of the queen ... a son was born ... without her suffering either pain or illness. ... When in due course he had issued from the womb, he appeared as if he had descended from the sky, for he did not come into the world through the portal of life; and, since he had purified his being through many an eons, he was born not ignorant but fully conscious. With his lustre and steadfastness, he appeared like the young sun that had come down to earth ... For with the glowing radiance of his limbs ... he illumined all the quarters of space (Johnston, 1972).

(The seven steps follow without previously mentioning the child being received by welcoming gods.)

The early texts were subject to several comments. Christian Luczanits discusses the period before the birth.

Prior to birth, it is said, the Bodhisattva had stayed in Tusita heaven and descended from there to assume his last worldly existence. Indeed, the notion that the last birth of a Buddha follows a sojourn in Tusita heaven, found in all textual sources that also narrate the birth. However, there are considerable differences in these sources, concerning the context of the descent from heaven and in the details narrated. In principle, the events prior to birth become more and more elaborate and miraculous (Luczanits, 1993, p. 41).

In the *Vinaya*s of the Mahīśāsaka and Dharmaguptaka schools, which are preserved in Chinese translations only, the birth of the Buddha is not narrated at all. Instead, these texts focus on the origin of the Śākya-clan, its genealogy and jump directly to the prophecy of the Brahmans. Obviously the Brahmans do not prophesize on the basis of Māyā's dream, since that is not narrated either.

In the canonical Pāli literature, there are only two works that also narrate the birth of the Buddha. These are the Mahāpadānasutta (MASU) of the DīghaNikāya, which is also partly preserved in a Sanskrit version (Mahāvadānasūtra), and the Acchariyabbhutadhammasutta. Both declare that the events during the last life of any Buddha are, as a matter of fact, identical (Luczanits, 1993, p. 43).

Nidāna-Kathā

Now between the two towns, there is a pleasure-grove of sāl-trees belonging to the people of both cities, and called the Lumbini grove. At that time, from the roots to the topmost branches, it was one mass of fruits and flowers; and amidst the blossoms and branches swarms of various-coloured bees, and flocks of birds of different kinds roamed warbling sweetly. The whole of the Lumbini grove was like a wood of variegated creepers, or the well-decorated banqueting hall of some mighty King. The Queen beholding it was filled with the desire of besporting herself in the sāl-tree grove; and the attendants carrying the Queen, entered the wood. When she came to the monarch sāl-tree of the glade, she wanted to take hold of its branch, and the branch bending down, like a reed heated by steam, approached within reach of her hand. Stretching out her hand, she took hold of the branch, and then karma-born winds shook her. Standing, and holding the branch of the sāl-tree, she delivered.

That very moment, the four pure-minded MahāBrahmās came there, bringing a golden net; and receiving the future Buddha on that net, they placed him before his mother, saying: 'Be joyful, O Lady! A mighty son is born to thee!'

Now other living things, when they leave their mother's womb, leave it smeared with offensive and impure matters. Not so the Bodhisattva. The future Buddha left his mother's womb like a preacher descending from a pulpit or a man from a ladder, erect, stretching out his hands and feet, unsoiled by any impurities from contact with his mother's womb, pure and fair, and shining like a gem placed on fine muslin of Benares. But though this was so, two showers of water came down from heaven in their honour and refreshed the Bodhisattva and his mother, and cleansed her body.

From the hands of the Brahmās, who had received him in the golden net, the Four Kings received him on cloth of antelope skins, soft to the touch, as are used on occasions of royal state. From their hands, men received him on a roll of fine cloth; and on leaving their hands, he stood up on the ground and looked towards the East. Thousands of world-systems became visible to him like a single open space. Men and devas, offering him sweet-smelling garlands, said: 'O great man, there is no other like thee, how then a greater?' Searching the 10 directions and finding no one like himself, he took seven strides, saying: 'This is the best direction.' And as he walked, the Great Brahmā held over him the white umbrella, and the Suyāma followed him with the fan, and other devas with other symbols of royalty in their hands. Then, stopping at the seventh step, he sent forth his noble voice and shouted the shout of victory, beginning with: 'I am the chief of the world.'

The Madurattha Vilāsini adds the rest, 'I am supreme in the world; this is my last birth; henceforth, there will be no rebirth for me' (Davids, 1880, pp.153-155).

As already mentioned by John Strong in his book, *The Buddha – A Short Biography*, we are not told much about Lord Buddha's actual birth.

In relatively early canonical sources, we are not told much about the Buddha's actual birth. From Tusita Heaven, he is simply said to descend and enter the side of his mother, Queen Māyā. He dwells in her womb for exactly ten lunar months, during which time he remains calm, alert, perfectly formed in body, and unsullied by any pollution. In some sources, Māyā is said to be able to see and contemplate him inside her. At the end of this period, she gives birth while standing up holding on to the branch of a tree. The birth is painless. The Buddha is not born naturally, but emerges from his mother's side. This lack of passage through the birth canal is often said to reflect a concern for purity, but it may also be connected to a pan-Indian tradition that asserts that the trauma of natural birth is what wipes out the memory of previous lives. In this context, since the Buddha is aware of his previous existences, he obviously could not have been born naturally.

Later biographical traditions were to draw out and expand upon this whole scenario — starting with the Buddha's conception. For instance, the Mahāyānist text Lalitavistara, which does not actually get to the Buddha's birth until its seventh chapter, dwells at first, and at great length, on his activities in Tusita Heaven, on his preparations for his final birth, his contemplation of the right time, place, family, and mother for that birth, and on his final teachings to his fellow gods in heaven, followed by his descent into his mother's womb in the form of a great six-tusked white elephant. Some traditions present this elephant merely as something dreamt by his mother. In either case, it is clearly an auspicious symbol of sovereignty (the great white elephant was one of the emblems of the cakravartin king), as well as a reference to one of the Jātaka tales which features the Bodhisattva's self-sacrifice as a great six-tusked elephant.

The Lalitavistara also describes at length the bodhisattva's intra-uterine life, portraying him as sitting on a divan that is soft as Benares silk and is set within a perfumed chamber, inside a bejewelled palace-like pavilion implanted in his mother's belly. Inside this amniotic chamber, the Buddha is said already to possess the thirty-two marks of the great man, and to receive various divinities, who come to visit him and hear him preach the Dharma. This whole placental palace, the text is careful to point out, in no way harms or brings discomfort to Queen Māyā, and, at the time of the Buddha's birth, it also emerges and is transported up to Brahmā's heaven, where it is worshipped as a relic. It is clear here that this text has moved very far away from the notion of an ordinary human birth.

The biographical tradition was to locate the event of the Buddha's birth in the village (or park) of Lumbinī, a site that was visited as early as the third century BCE by the emperor Asoka, and is located just north of the Indian border in what is now southern Nepal. The Pali commentaries explain that Queen Māyā wanted to have her child at her parent's house in Devadaha, but failed to make it all the way home in time, and so gave birth at Lumbini – the halfway point of her journey. A Sanskrit text develops this story further, maintaining that Lumbini was actually the name of Māyā's mother; the park in question was named for her after having been made by Māyā's father, Suprabuddha, at a point half-way between the towns of Devadaha and Kapilavastu.

As it is obvious from all nativity scenes, either in painting or in sculpture, the mother gave birth to the child standing up and holding the branch of a tree. This motif may have evolved from a pan-Indian motif 'the lady under the tree' (Strong, 2001, pp. 38-39).

The nativity scene, stone reliefs, Borobudur

Latitavistara

Lord, please listen to what is on my mind;
For a long time now, I have thought about the pleasure grove.
If you will not be upset, displeased, or envious,
I should quickly go to that pleasure grove.

You are also weary from austerities and diligently contemplating the Dharma;
I myself have carried a pure being within me for a long time now.
The sāla, that most wonderful of trees, is now in blossom;
O Lord, it is therefore fitting for us to go to the pleasure grove!

Spring, that excellent season, is a joyous time for women;
The bees are humming and the cuckoos singing.
Fresh and sweet, the fragrance of flowers drifts through the air;
Please issue an order, and let us go there right away!

The king heard Māyādevī's words, and then,
Delighted and elated, he spoke to his retinue:
Arrange my horses, elephants, and chariots!
Decorate the excellent garden at Lumbinī!

Quick, prepare twenty thousand elephants,
Dark blue like mountains or storm clouds. [79]
Ornament the lordly six-tusked elephants with bells attached to their flanks;
Decorate them with gold and gems and cover them with lattices of gold.

Quick, harness twenty thousand royal steeds,
Fast as the wind, strong and excellent steeds,
With silvery snow-colored tails, manes that are beautifully plaited,
And lattices of golden bells hung on their flanks.

Have Lumbinī bestrewn with gold and jewels;
Adorn all the trees with many types of cloths and jewels.
Quick, plant many flowers, like in the gardens of the gods;
Arrange all of this, and then swiftly report to me.

Hearing this, the retinue immediately arranged
All the conveyances and ornamented Lumbinī.
They then called out, 'Victory! Victory! Long live the king!
Your command is fulfilled and all is ready. Please look, O lord!'

(Translating the Words of the Buddha)

The narrative of the birth of the Buddha

[I]

Then, when the eighth day of the first month, [that is] the time of the birth, had come, there manifested in the park of King Śuddhodana 32 omens. All flowers, the lotuses in the ponds and the blossoms on the trees of paradise opened up, but then they ripened no further. Eight trees of paradise bearing precious jewels grew up, [and] 20,000 treasure mines were laid bare; in the houses precious jewels sprouted forth. With a dash of perfumed water, all the defilements of the swollen water channels were purified, by reason of its fragrant scent. The lion cubs, which had descended from the snow ranges, circumambulated the town of Kapilavastu, and afterwards did not cause harm to any living being, as they lay at the gates [of the town]. Five hundred ashen-grey elephant calves arrived and touched the King's feet with the tip of their trunks.

Divine children rolled about in the laps of the retinue of the wife of King Śuddhodana, nāgā girls charged with offering articles emerged [from the ground] with half of their bodies and roamed the sky, and 10,000 divine girls decorated with peacock feathers hovered in the sky. And 10,000 filled vessels encircled Kapilavastu [as well]. Divine girls stood by with golden vessels filled to the brim with globules of perfumed water. Ten thousand divine girls stood by with umbrellas and flags. Many hundreds [and] thousands of divine girls set down conch shells, drums and the like from their necks and took up their places.

Wind and dust did not rise; no rivers flowed or moved about. The sun, moon and the stars did not wander [through the sky]. The lunar mansion (naksatra) [known as] sKar-ma rgyal [held sway]. The house of Śuddhodana was covered with a net of precious jewels. Not even a fire was burning [in it]. Glittering gems and precious jewels hung from the two-storeyed palace, and its golden roof and its toranas. Doors opened up onto treasure stores full of calico and manifold precious jewels. There was no noise from owls or the like; [only] pleasant voices were to be heard. The broad stream of the acts (karma) of the beings had been severed. All regions were flat, [and] the crossroads and the centres of the market places were strewn with snippets of flowers. Pregnant women gave birth with pleasure.

The deities inhabiting the groves of sāl trees emerged with half of their bodies from the leaves of the trees and bowed down in respect, and [arboral] residences appeared.

[II]

Then, because the Bodhisattva had for a long time been uttering praises of seclusion and had been happy in anticipation of it, and because the gods could make no offerings if he were born in the town [of Kapilavastu], and also because the Śākya clan would manifest indecent behaviour, the thought arouse in Māyādevī, who realized that the time had come for the birth of the Bodhisattva, of proceeding to the seclusion of the grove of Lumbinī and staying [there].

In the twilight of the evening, she approached the King and spoke: 'As I have been wishing for a long time to go to the grove of Lumbinī, give your unreserved permission [to do so]!' The King himself, after he had fully awoken [the next day], ordered that the grove of Lumbinī be cleaned. At that time, great omens appeared in the grove: phenomena occurred in all the jewelled palaces above the earth, and light burst forth from all the petals of the opened jewelled lotuses and covered [everything], accompanied by the sound: 'He will be born!' And in the grove, 10 appearances — including those of the Jinaputras of the 10 directions — manifested, generating the 'Mind [of Enlighten¬ment]' (bodhicitta) up to 'Enlightenment' (bodhi).

[III]

Then, when King Śuddhodana had furnished his own retinue with oxen, horses and 20,000 guards and had ordered that the grove of Lumbinī be beautified with ornaments, he spoke to the women of the retinue of the Queen: 'Decorate yourself with ornaments and bind cymbals [on your hands]! Order the best of carriages to be available — similar to a magic unicorn. Let the younger women pull it!'

After the women had acted accordingly, Māyā [devī] and her retinue set off. When they approached the gate [of Kapilavastu], the great sound of an assembly of a 100,000 beings arose — the ringing of a 100,000 ritual bells [to cause] joy. On the carriage adorned with precious jewels, four bejewelled trees of paradise were set up, bearing blossoms and leaves. The whole was covered with a net of ritual bells and divine cloth, [let down] from above by peacocks, geese and swans. A lion throne with umbrellas, victory banners and flags erected over it was prepared by the deities, [and] as soon as the mother sat down, the earth moved.

The gods scattered flowers from the sky and exclaimed: 'Today the Noble One among the beings will be born!' The four 'Protectors of the world' (lokapāla) guided the carriage, Indra cleaned the way, Brahma cleared it, and 100,000 gods went along, bowing down in respect.

Behind the carriage of the Queen [were] horse [and] elephant carriages, encircled and protected by 84,000 armoured guards. Sixty million girls of the Śākya [family] went ahead, [and the carriage] was encircled by 60,000 persons playing cymbals and singing songs. Divine, nāgā, gandharva, kinnara and asura girls — 48,000 each — followed behind, singing songs and uttering praises. The King himself observed this from his residence of Kapilavastu and thought: 'This son will surely become an Enlightened One!'

The grove of Lumbinī itself was anointed with perfumed water and strewn with godly flowers, [while] on trees of paradise grew unseasonal leaves, blossoms and fruits. The order was given to adorn them with red silk, [and] they were [also] covered with ornaments of gold and precious jewels.

[IV]

Then, after Māyādevī had arrived at the grove of Lumbinī, she descended from the carriage. Encircled by Umā [i.e. Śiva's consort], old women of human origin, 60,000 divine girls and a throng of [other] beings, she went from wood to wood and wandered from forest to forest — slowly moving on, looking from one tree to another. And in a wide, flat area full of blue[-green] grass, touching which one became joyous, grew Aśoka [trees] adorned with flowers, joyful sāl trees, and the tree called plaksa, a King among trees — which had [already] supported mothers of earlier Jinas, being a tree honoured by the gods of the pure realms. Its root blazed forth with the light of the most precious jewels, its trunk, branches and leaves were adorned with precious jewels, its manifold earthly and divine blossoms were in bloom, endowed with the aroma of excellent perfume, [and] on it was hanging multi-coloured silk. When she arrived there, immediately the branches of these trees of paradise bowed down and greeted her in respect of the Bodhisattva [carried by her].

At that time, all the light of the 3,000 [worlds] was outshone by the appearance of the light coming forth from all the gates of the body hair of Māyādevī, and the suffering and obscuration of the [three] lower realms came to rest. [This light] entered the body of the [three] thousand great worlds, and it appeared, as if separately, near a tree in a park of the manifold royal residences of the 10 milliards Jambudvīpas of these [worlds], being present individually [as many] Māyādevīs. And in each and every body hair appeared [as performed] by the Bodhisattva, the [different] ways of making offerings as many earlier Jinas as there were, and as much of the doctrine as was propounded [by them] was uttered. Similarly, all the earlier deeds of the Bodhisattva, the endless Buddha-fields in their entirety and as many implements as were used, appeared in the grove of Lumbinī.

[V]

In order to demonstrate a joyous birth, the mother extended her right arm, and after grasping a branch of the plaksa [tree], she gazed into the centre of the sky and stretched herself. At that time, numerous enjoyable sensations of the Bodhisattva, transcending [those] of the gods, arose from the womb of the mother, and the many Buddhas similar to Śākyamuni came forth. Offerings in the form of Kingly eight-petalled lotuses of precious jewels made from Vajras manifested in front of the mother.

Śatakratu [= Indra] pondered: 'As this mother is endowed with a sense of shame, she is not able to give birth amidst so many people. And as she also shies away from me, I must at all costs scatter her retinue, and personally seize the Bodhisattva [after his birth]!' He then made a violent hail shower come down, whereupon the multitudes of the retinue ran away. Śatakratu put on the garments of an old woman [those of] his own mother, and sat down near [Māyādevī]. Brahma was present as well.

Then all the Tathāgathas made light come forth, so as to induce the Bodhisattva to take birth. And so that the doubts [of those who might think that] all these sentient Bodhisattvas had been born from an embryo produced by a father and a mother might be sundered, and that something pure and very excellent might be demonstrated, he was born in the midnight hour from the right side of the mother's ribs in a state of full consciousness, while a light which frightened enemies and [caused] joy if touched spread, having the appearance of gold, in the expanse of the 3,000 [worlds]. He was endowed with the 10 aspects of birth, the [moon] at the time [still] being in [the mansion] sKar-ma rgyal.

In order to fulfil the earlier prayer and to make the other gods feel craving, Śatakratu covered his hands with a layer of animal hide and seized [the Bodhisattva] with a layer of precious divine material from Kāśi [i.e. Benares]. To subdue Śatakratu's pride, the Bodhisattva empowered his body as a vajra so that he was not able to seize him. When Śatakratu was trembling [with fear], [the Bodhisattva] spoke: 'Kauśika, let me go! Leave me!' Brahma, [too, tried to] seize [the Bodhisattva] with the layer of divine material from Kāśi, but he was not able to hold either; and so he carried away the two-storied palace used [by the Bodhisattva] in order to venerate it in Brahmaloka. It is known that the four Great Kings [i.e. the Protectors of the world] wanted to seize [the Bodhisattva] [as well], but could not hold him. [Only] after four Godly Sons had been established in the four cardinal directions, could he be held with the layer of wild animal hide; this was done, in short, so that he did not suddenly plunge onto the ground.

At that time, the blossoms of all trees unfolded and fruits came forth. There was a rain of flowers, the stream of the three lower realms was interrupted, all living beings were no longer harmed by their obscurations, beings without their senses possessed them [from this time onwards], [and] the earth moved.

[VI]

At that moment, when the Bodhisattva had taken birth, in four great towns, sons were born to four kings as well. When in Śrāvastī the son of King Brahmadatta Aranemi was born, he appeared as had been clear to the divinators of the country that he would, and thus, his name was Prasenajit. When in Rajagrihā the son of King Mahāpadma was born, he appeared in the shape of the rising sun and was the son of a beautiful woman; therefore, he was called Bimbisāra. When in Kauśambī the son of King Śatanīka was born, he appeared like the rising sun of the world; therefore he was called Udayana. When in Ujjayinī, the son of King Anantanemi was born, he was like the brightness of the beacon of the world; therefore, he was called Pradyota. Each of these [Kings] was proud of the qualities of his own son.

At that time, in the town of the Śākyas [i.e. Kapilavastu]: 500 excellent ones were born, including Bhadrika Nanda, 500,000 further [members] of the Śākya [family], 800 subjects, including the one [named] Chanda, 10,000 girls of the Śākya [family], including the one [named] Praśansa, 800 female servants, 20,000 girls of royal origin, and from Brahmin and householder [castes], 20,000 male and female horses, including the famous white riding horse that emits golden light [Kasthaka], 10,000 excellent elephants [and] 6,000 male and female oxen. Twenty thousand elephants adorned with gold trumpeted from the sky and came to Kapilavastu. Also, [he who is called] Udayin, the son of Udayana, a minister of Śuddhodana, was born.

[VII]

Blossoms opened up on the trunk of aśvata [trees] in the centre of Jambudvīpa, and udumbara [lotuses] on the shore of [Lake] Anavaptata. Corals sprouted in the sandalwood groves and on the mountain peaks of the minor continents. On the banks of the falling torrent Lohita the tree known as Virtuous Essence grew a 100 cubits in one day: as long as the sun has not arisen, it can be cut with a finger nail; [but] after the sun has risen, not even fire can burn it.

In the grove of Lumbinī, a *stūpa* similar to a heap of lotuses was erected— known as the 'Caitya where [the Buddha] was born'. Five hundred parks, including [the one known as] Stainless Array, and also 500 treasures, appeared for the enjoyment of the Bodhisattva. For their part, 20,000 minor royal domains offered taxes and bowed before him.

As told by sKal-bzang Chos-kyi rgya-mtsho (fifteenth century). Translation from the Tibetan original by Franz-Karl Ehrhard from the 'Treasure of the Conduct in the Form of Unerring Deeds', the third chapter, called, 'The Deed of the Birth' (Cüppers, et al., 2010, pp. 362-369).

'Lumbini, where I was born'

At the age of 80, before Lord Buddha passed away in Kushinagara, he said to his faithful disciple Ananda:

> There are four places, Ananda, that a pious person should visit and look upon with feelings of reverence. What are the four?
>
> 'Here the Tathagata was born!'[Lumbini] This, Ananda, is a place that a pious person should visit and look upon with feelings of reverence.
>
> 'Here the Tathagata became fully enlightened in unsurpassed, supreme Enlightenment!'[Bodhgaya] This, Ananda, is a place that a pious person should visit and look upon with feelings of reverence.
>
> 'Here the Tathagata set rolling the unexcelled Wheel of the Dhamma!'[Sarnath] This, Ananda, is a place that a pious person should visit and look upon with feelings of reverence.
>
> 'Here the Tathagata passed away into the state of Nibbana in which no element of clinging remains!' [Kusinara] This, Ananda, is a place that a pious person should visit and look upon with feelings of reverence.
>
> These, Ananda, are the four places that a pious person should visit and look upon with feelings of reverence. And truly there will come to these places, Ananda, pious bhikkhus and bhikkhunis, laymen and laywomen, reflecting: 'Here the Tathagata was born! Here the Tathagata became fully enlightened in unsurpassed, supreme Enlightenment! Here the Tathagata set rolling the unexcelled Wheel of the Dhamma! Here the Tathagata passed away into the state of Nibbana in which no element of clinging remains!'
>
> 'And whoever, Ananda, should die on such a pilgrimage with his heart established in faith, at the breaking up of the body, after death, will be reborn in a realm of heavenly happiness.'
>
> (Maha-parinibbana Sutta: Last Days of the Buddha (DN 16), translated from the Pali by Sister Vajira & Francis Story, Part 5 lines 16 to 22)

From the sources above, it appears that the concept of Lumbini as the birth place of Lord Buddha was established during the formation of Buddhist canonical literature. It developed from the notion of a simple forest or garden to a celestial place as depicted in the late sutras. From the above information, we must conclude that a more precise picture of Lumbini has to be provided by archaeological research in and around Lumbini. It is not a surprise that Kenzo Tange left the core of the Sacred Garden area out of his Master Plan design. Instead, he pointed out that the design of the Sacred Garden should only be carried out after the archaeological excavations were completed. The Sacred Garden would be an area which represents the scene of Lord Buddha's birthplace and in which all the archaeological remains of the site would be integrated into the pilgrims' *Pradakshina Walk*. This approach would fulfil the aspiration of all pilgrims who come to Lumbini for worship, to a place which Lord Buddha himself designated as a sacred site.

© UNESCO/Dhan K. Limbu

Circular pond around the Scared Garden in Lumbini

Perception Two

Because the Buddha was born here. Lumbini in historical texts

There are a number of historical sources relevant to Lumbini. Two inscriptions found on the Ashoka Pillar range from the third century BCE to the fourteenth century CE. The early historical documentation of the site is limited to the sketchy texts written by Chinese travellers such as Zhi Sengzai (350-375 CE), Faxian (409 CE) and Xuanzang (636 CE). After the 'rediscovery' of Lumbini in 1896 information on Lumbini was recorded by visitors and researchers.

Content

Historical records. After the *mahāparinirvāna* of Lord Buddha. Emperor Ashoka's pilgrimage. Accounts by Chinese travellers. Pilgrimage of Ripu Malla. Visitors after 1896. Involvement of the United Nations.

References

This chapter is based on contributions by Basanta Bidari. References are also attributed to Robin Coningham and Christoph Cüppers.

Historical records

When Lord Buddha was approaching his *mahāparinirvāna,* he advised his followers that there were four great places of pilgrimage associated with his life: Lumbini, where he was born; Bodh Gaya, where he achieved enlightenment; Sarnath, where he first taught the Dharma; and Kushinagara, where he achieved his *mahāparinirvāna* or great passing (Beal, 1983, p. 126). From that time, Lumbini became an important pilgrimage site for early Buddhists, as reflected by Ashoka's own pilgrimage in 249 BCE, marked as it was on an inscribed pillar.

It is also clear that the appeal of the site stretched beyond South Asia, as exemplified by the pilgrimage of numerous Chinese monks; the two most famous being Faxian in the fifth century CE and Xuanzang in the seventh century CE, whose accounts were later used by antiquarians in the nineteenth century in an attempt to locate the site (Coningham, 2001, p. 63).

Ashoka's Pillar also contains the fourteenth century CE graffiti of Prince Ripu Malla, demonstrating that Lumbini remained a key site into the medieval period. Indeed, the various stages of construction are proof that the site remained an important place of pilgrimage from the Mauryan period onwards with multiple phases of building and remodelling. However, it is also clear that detailed knowledge of the site was lost between the pilgrimage of Ripu Malla and Lumbini's re-identification in 1896.

From the beginning, Western scholars of Buddhism were eager to find the non-textual proof of the life of Lord Buddha and the events described in the relevant Buddhist texts. In their hunt for the historical places of Lord Buddha, archaeologists and scholars in the service of the British colonial government had to wait until the end of the ninteenth and the beginning of the twentieth century when the discoveries of artefacts with clear inscriptional evidence revealed to them the places, in which Buddhist tradition ascribed the most important stages of the life of their founder. One of the finest monographs that sought to bring together the textual, art, historical and archaeological evidence is certainly Foucher in 1949. While the locations of Lord Buddha's enlightenment and first sermon were identified quite early on, the question of where Lord Buddha entered into *parinirvāna* – Kushinagara – and where he was born and grew up –

Lumbinī and Kapilavastu – were not solved until the end of the ninteenth century (Härtel, 1991 and Falk, 1998).

As to the last two places, this happened when the two Ashokan inscriptions, one in Nigāli Sāgar near Tilaurakot referring to the Buddha of the past, Konakamuni (Kanakamuni) and one in Lumbini were found. This discovery made it very clear that this area had been a region closely connected to the early life of Lord Buddha – to his birth and his youth – in a period of less than 200 years after his *parinirvāna*. This delivered concrete proof that in the Mauryan period the place, where the Lumbini Pillar stands, was indeed considered to be the original and authentic birthplace of Lord Buddha (Deeg, 2003).

Ashoka Pillar

After the *mahāparinirvāna* of Lord Buddha

After the *mahāparinirvāna* of Lord Buddha, Lumbini became an important site for Buddhist pilgrimage near and far, witnessing a continuous flow of people, who came with faith and devotion, seeking purification of their minds. The birthplace has yielded ample cultural deposits belonging to the fifth and sixth centuries BCE. There is however no record or evidence of visits made by any high authorities before Emperor Ashoka visited in the third century BCE.

Over the following centuries numerous visitors to Lumbini recorded their observations. The records that have been salvaged and translated are from Chinese Buddhist monks who travelled to where Buddhism originated from. Here they hoped to find the true and authentic teachings to revive their faith.

> However, China was not destined to receive Buddhism nor to see it propagated by apostles who came from India. This nation, which seems to do everything in an inverted order, far from waiting for the religious faith to be brought to it, went to seek for it in foreign lands. It was as it were proselytism reversed. The Chinese pilgrims, for they cannot be called missionaries, went to India, some thousands miles from their own country, to imbibe a purer dogma or to revive a failing faith (Saint-Hilaire, 1952, p. 4).

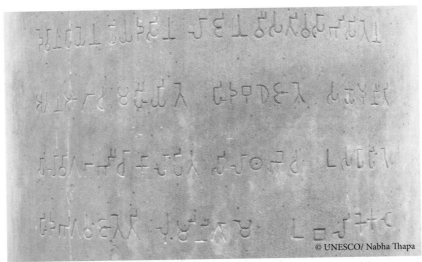

Inscription on the Ashoka Pillar

Emperor Ashoka's pilgrimage

The third century BCE is a landmark era in the history of Lumbini. The conversion of Emperor Ashoka after the massacre and bloodshed in the devastating battle of Kalinga (present-day Orissa state in India) was a milestone in the history of Buddhism.

According to Buddhist tradition, as preserved in the Divyavadana, Ashoka started on a pilgrimage to Lumbini in the company of his preceptor, Upagupta. On their arrival, Upagupta, pointing to the tree under which the mother of the Buddha had stood holding on to a branch while delivering her child, said, 'Oh, Maharaja! Here the Blessed One was born'. To commemorate his visit he left behind monuments to propagate the Dhamma (the teachings of the Buddha) (Przyluski, 1967, pp. 29-30).

In Lumbini, he erected a sandstone pillar with an inscription to memorialize his visit in 249 BCE The inscription contains five lines and 90 letters (Brahmi script and the language Pali, though according to some scholars, it is in the Ardha Magadhi, an ancient form of Magadhi Prakrit and often considered synonymous with Pali). The inscription reads as follows:

> Devānapiyena Piyadasina lājina vīsativasābhisitena
> atana āgāca mahīyite hida Budhe jāte Sakyamuniti
> silāvigadabhīcā kālāpite silāthabecha usapāpite
> hida Bhagavam jāte ti Lummini gāme ubalike kate
> athabhāgiye ca (Japanese Buddhist Federation, 2001, pp. 74-75).

The first statement proclaims: *King Piyadasi, the beloved of the gods, in the twentieth year of his reign, personally came to pay reverence.* There are variations in the words used in the different translations; however the meaning of this phrase is clear. This is followed by the statement: *Since the Buddha Sakyamuni was born here* ... testimony to this being the birthplace of Siddhartha Gautama.

The parts that follow seem to have been more difficult to translate, especially the two phrases: *silā vigadabhī cā* and *ubalike kate athabhāgiye ca*. The king has donated various stone objects due to the fact that Sakyamuni Buddha was born here. The second part of this line clearly states that a stone pillar was erected. The translation of the first part however varies greatly between the interpretations that a stone railing was constructed or that it refers to a stone figure possibly even that of the supposed horse capital mentioned by Xuanzang, the Chinese traveller, who visited Lumbini in the seventh century. The interpretation to this phrase has changed after the Marker Stone was found in 1994. A.K. Narain suggests that it could mean 'a public assemblage area in the form of a high terrace or an enclosure of bricks, *bhīcā*, around a place of worship or celebration (mahiyite) of the much spoken of (unusual stone) (*silāvigada*)' (Japanese Buddhist Federation, 2001, p. 25). Keisho Tsukamoto, a professor emeritus at Tohoku University and specialist in Indology and the history of Buddhism proposes that the term refers to the Marker Stone: 'He caused to be made [the structure] with the enclosure (or wall) [to protect] the stone being in its natural condition, i.e. a piece of natural rock...' (Japanese Buddhist Federation, 2005, p. 20)

The last part of the inscription states: *The Lord having been born here, the Lumbini village has been exempted of taxes and granted the eight shares or reduced the tax to an eighth part (from the usual sixth).* The interpretation that there is reference of granting the eight rights is proposed by Harry Falk (1998, p. 20).

An English translation of the inscription would be as follows:

> By King Piyadasi, the beloved of the gods (who) having been consecrated twenty years (having) come himself personally (here) to offer homage, or celebrate, because Shakyamuni Buddha was born here, was caused both a Silavigadabhica to be built and a stone pillar to be set up. (And), because the Lord was born here, the Lumbini village was made free from taxes and liable to pay (only) one-eighth part (of the produce) (Japanese Buddhist Federation, 2001, p. 75).

From the inscription of the Ashoka Pillar in Lumbini, it can be concluded that Ashoka showed his respect for the Buddha. He personally visited Lumbini, worshipped at the birth spot and constructed a platform to place the Marker Stone upon and erected a stone pillar with a suitable inscription stating the significance of the place as one worthy of commemoration. The inscription also states that pilgrims visiting the location were exempt from all religious taxes and that the levy on the produce of the village of Lumbini was reduced.

Accounts by Chinese travellers

Zhi Sengzai

The Yuchi-monk Zhi Sengzai (Seng Tsai) of the Chin Dynasty (265 - 420 CE) is known to be the first Chinese person to visit Lumbini, between 350 - 375 CE.

The account in the *Shui-Ching-Chu* (Shuijing-zhu) provides more information about Lumbini during Zhi Sengzai's visits. The following is a translation from Zhi Sengzai's lost Waiguo-shi in the Shuijing-zhu, anterior to 400 CE.

> Waiguo-shi says that the kingdom of Kapilavastu (Jiaweiluoyue) does not have a king now. The city and its ponds are deserted and dirty, there being only an empty space. There are some upāsaka, about 20 households of the Shākya family; they are the descendants of King Shuddhodana. Of old they formed four families, who dwelt inside the old city and lived as upāsakas; formerly they zealously cultivated religious energy (*vīrya*) and still maintained the old spirit. In those days, when the *stūpas* were dilapidated, they completely repaired them. The King of Kapilavastu, over and above this, took care of one *stūpa*, and the king of Sidha (la) dvīpa (Sihetiao) sent gifts as an aid to finish it. But now there are [only] 12 monks who dwell inside the [city].

> The marvellous tree, which the excellent queen grasped when the Buddha was being born, is called *xuhe* (a) shoka. King Ashoka made a statue of the queen, in the act of grasping [the tree] and giving birth to the prince, out of lapis lazuli. When the old tree had no more offshoots, all the *shramata* took the old trunk and planted it; and over and over again it continued itself till the present time. The branches of the tree still shelter the stone statue.

> The outlines of the marks where the prince walked seven steps are also still preserved today. King Ashoka enclosed the marks with lapis lazuli on both sides, and again had them covered over with one long slab of lapis lazuli. The people of the country continually make offerings to them with sweet-smelling flowers. One still clearly sees the outlines of the seven footprints; although there is no slab covering them, it makes no difference. And again, people may cover them with several layers of heavy cotton (*karpāsa*), fastening the latter to the chiselled stone but still [the marks] shine through them and are even brighter than before.

> When the prince was born, the (two) kings of the *nāgas* came to the prince and, one to the left and the other to the right, spewed water and bathed him.

The one *nāga* was seen to spew cold water, and the other warm water; [this water] produced two pools. Even now, one pool is cold and the other is warm (Deeg, 2003, p. 56-57).

The account in the *Shui-Ching-Chu* further states that 'When the old tree had no more offshoots, all the *Sramanas* took the old trunk and planted it; and over and over again it continued to propagate itself till the present time' (Petech, 1950, p. 35).

The sacred pond with remains of ancient stupas

Faxian

Faxian, a Buddhist monk native in the Shansi province in China, came to Lumbini at the beginning of the fifth century CE. An excerpt of translations of his travel account concerning Lumbini is given below:

Going less than one yojana from there to the north, one comes to (another) township. This is the birthplace of the Buddha Kanakamuni [...], the place where father and son met and the place (where this Buddha) entered into *parinirvāna*; at all (these places) too, *stūpas* were erected.

Going less than one *yojana* from there to the east, one comes to the city of Kapilavastu ... In the whole city there is neither king nor population (left) and there are many mounds (of debris?) and much destruction. Only (a few) monks and ten families are living there. Where once stood the palace of King Suddhodana a statue of the prince's mother was erected (showing her) at the time when the prince, riding on a white elephant, entered her womb. ...

Fifty *li* to the east of the city there is a royal park. The park is called Lumbini (Lunmin). (There) the wife (of the king) took a bath in a pond, left the pond from the north side, took twenty steps forward, grasped a tree with her hand and, (turning) to the east, delivered the prince. The prince came down to the earth and took seven steps. The two *nāga* kings bathed the prince. On the spot where (his) body was washed, a well was built, and from the above-mentioned pond in which (the prince's mother) bathed, the monks still drink today.

The kingdom of Kapilavastu is barren and empty, the population is low, (and) on the roads one (has reason) to fear white elephants (and) lions. It is not easy to travel there (Deeg, 2003, pp. 46-48).

Note is also taken of the actual Ashoka tree which Mayadevi took hold of during her delivery was still living. (Beal, 1993, p. 88)

Painted specially for this work.
FA HSIEN AT THE RUINS OF ASOKA'S PALACE, A.D. 407.
The Chinese Buddhist monk Fa Hsien was the first of a long series of monastic visitors from China to India between the fifth and eighth centuries. In 407 he visited Pataliputra (Patna) with three followers, and has left an account of the Palace of Asoka which was then standing.

Public domain

Xuanzang

Public domain

In the seventh century CE Xuanzang, the most important pilgrim monk visited Lumbini. He left detailed descriptions of Lumbini in his travel account, as follows, he calls Lumbini the 'La-fa-ni' grove (Watters, 1973, p. 15).

Outside of the southern city gate, on the left side of the road, there is a *stūpa* (which marks the place where) the prince tried his skills with the Sākya in shooting (arrows) at iron drums. From there some 30 *li* to the south-east there is a *stūpa*; at the side of it there is a spring. The (water of the) spring flows clearly. This is (the place where) the prince compared his strength and matched his skills with the Sākya, (and when he) drew (the bow and) the arrow left (the string), it pierced the surfaces of the drums (and) flew further and penetrated into the soil (until its) feathers disappeared; from (the place where the arrow penetrated the earth) sprang a clear flow (of water). There is a common tradition which calls this (spot) the 'Arrow Spring' ... (When people) are sick (they) drink (this water) or bathe (in it and) are very often cured. People from far away carry the mud (of this spring) home, and depending on their sufferings smear it on their forehead, (for example). (As it is) mysteriously protected by the good spirits (it) often heals (the diseases).

Going eighty or ninty *li* north-east from the Arrow Spring, one comes to Lumbini. There is a bathing pond of the Sakya clan, (whose water is) clear as a mirror, and on whose surface flowers are scattered and drift. Twenty-four or twenty five steps to the north (of the pond), there is an Ashoka flower tree (Wuyou-hua-shu), which has now already withered; this is the place where the sacred birth of the Bodhisattva took place.

After the Bodhisattva was born, he took seven steps in each of the four cardinal directions without being supported and said: 'In heaven and on earth, I alone am the venerable. From now on, my rebirths have come to an end'. Big lotus flowers sprang up at the spots where he had set his feet. The two *nāgas* leapt out (from the earth) and rested in the air. Each of them spewed to wash the prince — one cold, one warm. East of the *stūpa* which (marks) the place where the prince was bathed, are two pure springs, and beside them two *stūpas* were built. This is the place where the two *nāgas* leapt out from the earth. After the Bodhisattva was born, the servants and relatives rushed to look for water to bathe (him). Two springs sprang up in front of the consort (Māyā) — one cold and one warm — in which (the prince) was bathed. To the south (of this place), there is a *stūpa* (which marks) the place where the ruler of the gods, Shakra, received the bodhisattva. When the Bodhisattva left his mother's womb, the ruler of the gods, Shakra, held up the Bodhisattva while kneeling on a marvellous, heavenly piece of cloth. Nearby there are four *stūpas*; this is the place where the four heavenly kings (lokapāla) took the Bodhisattva in their arms. When the Bodhisattva was born from the right thigh (of his mother), the four heavenly kings received the Bodhisattva in a piece of golden cloth, set him on a golden stand in front of his mother and said, 'The consort has given birth to that blessed child. She must indeed be happy! All the gods rejoice — how much more (will) mankind (rejoice)!

Beside the *stūpas* of the four heavenly kings, who took the prince in their arms, not far away, there is a big stone pillar (*da-shizhu*), (and) on top of it (they) have made a horse statue (*maxiang*); it was erected by King Asoka. Later an evil *nāga's* ferocious thunder-clap split the pillar in the middle down to the earth. At its side, there is a small river flowing south-east (which) is called in the local tradition 'Oil River' (You-he). After Lady Māyā had delivered (the child), the gods transformed the (original) lake into a shining and pure (pond of water) in order to deliver bath water for the lady so that she could get rid of her inner and outer infirmities. It has now become a (flowing) river, but its flowing (water) is usually pinguid.

From there, going eastward about 500 li (through) devastated fields and wild forests, (one) reaches the country of Rāma (grāma) (Lanmo) (in the region of Middle India). (Deeg, 2003, pp. 50-55).

Other Chinese Visitors

After a small interval of time, other visitors from China arrived, among them Wu-Kong and Fang Chi, who mention a great tope (stupa) at the spot, where the Lord Buddha was born. It was visited by Wu-Kong in about 764 CE. Xuanzang mentions the stone pillar, but does not say anything about the inscription on it. Fang Chi, however, tells us that the pillar recorded the circumstances of Lord Buddha's birth (Watters, 1973, p. 17).

Pilgrimage of Ripu Malla

On the uppermost portion on the eastern side of the Ashoka Pillar is an inscription from the beginning of the fourteenth century CE. This is the testimony of the last visitor to make a pilgrimage to Lumbini before it was lost and forgotten in the jungles for the following five centuries. Ripu Malla, a Prince of the Nagaraja dynasty of western Nepal, got his name and a prayer engraved. The inscription reads:

Om Mani Padme Hum
Sri Ripu Malla Chidam Jayatu
Sangrama Malla

© Kai Weise

Ripu Malla inscription

The first phrase is a Mahayana Buddhist prayer, followed by the phrase which means: 'May Prince Malla be long victorious'. This indicates that up to the time of Ripu Malla, Lumbini and Kapilavastu were widely known as the birthplace and homeland of Lord Buddha.

Lumbini, the most important sacred place of Buddhist pilgrimage, was slowly converted into bush land and faded from memory for a long time after the visit of Ripu Malla. Some scholars link this fact to the revival of Hinduism and the Muslim invasions. Others have suggested that natural disasters, such as drought, famine, floods in the rainy season, or earthquakes caused people to abandon Lumbini. However, little research is available and it would be a worthwhile undertaking to further study the history of Lumbini from the fourteenth to the nineteenth century before the rediscovery of Lumbini.

The religious confusion of medieval times brought damage and neglect to Buddhist sacred places of pilgrimage. The association of Lumbini with Lord Buddha was slowly forgotten. But the Buddha's great message survived, growing in importance through the centuries (Pradhan, 1979, pp. 30-32).

Visitors after 1896

It was on 1 December 1896 when General Khadga Shamsher Rana and archaeologist Anton Führer visited Lumbini for the first time. Subsequently the Ashoka Pillar in Lumbini was rediscovered and the inscription was deciphered. Anton Führer's accounts have been published under the title: *Antiquities of Buddha Sakyamuni's Birthplace in the Nepalese Tarai* (1972)

Anagarika Dhammapala of Sri Lanka together with P. C. Jinavaravamsa, the Prince of Thailand, visited Lumbini on 6 April 1898. They described the mound, covered with bushes with the pillar protruding eight to ten feet high. They provide a rough description of the pillar, the materials, dimensions and inscriptions. The image of Mayadevi (Nativity Sculpture) was kept in a temple comprising of a single small room several feet into the mound some fifteen feet east of the pillar supposedly erected by the Government of Nepal. The access, which required descending down some steps, was guarded by a Gurkha guard of Nepal. Supposedly a Chinese Buddhist Lama was taking care of the image. However Hindu pilgrims offered *puja* and animal sacrifices to the image that they considered to be of Rumindevi, a form of Bhagvati or Durga.

According to Dhammapal, in April 1898, N. Sadananda, the Residence Priest of the Mahabodhi Society of Calcutta, Sylvain Levi and Anton Führer also visited Lumbini. They also travelled to Kapilavastu, where excavations were being carried out under the supervision of Anton Führer (Dhammapal, 1898, p. 17).

Purna Chandra Mukherji conducted a brief exploration and excavation visit in 1899. He identified the Saptaratha, the seven-bayed temple from the Gupta period and the sculpture with the nativity motive (Mukherji, 1969).

Ekai Kawaguchi, a Japanese monk, who took a pilgrimage through Nepal into Tibet in the early twentieth century, visited Lumbini in 1912. Abhi Subedi, in his book *Ekai Kawaguchi: The Trespassing Insider* explains how Kawaguchi vehemently opposed the sacrificing of animals in Lumbini and lodged a complaint to the Prime Minister Chandra Shamsher Rana. Accordingly the practice was stopped (Subedi, 1999, p. 135).

Alexandra David-Neel, another adventurer visited Lumbini and Kapilvastu in December 1913 supposedly on the invitation from the King of Nepal, facilitated by Tibetologist Charles Bell and at the time a British political officer in Sikkim. He spent a night in Tilaurakot, which was populated by man-eating tigers (Foster, 1998, p. 100).

According to the personal visitor book of Vishnu Prasad Chaudhari, former landlord and chairperson of the Village Development Committee in Khungai, Lumbini, as well as the famous Indian scholars, Rahul Sankrityayana, Ramesh Chandra Majumdar and Ramkrishna Mukherji, visited Lumbini in the 1920s.

Keshar Shamsher Rana carried out major excavation work between 1933 and 1939. His main aim was the beautification of the site by levelling the ground, exposing some of the ancient structures, building a new temple for the nativity statue and enlarging the pool with brick steps. There are however no documents on the activities carried out by Keshar Shamsher Rana other than a few photographs.

Italian explorer Giuseppe Tucci visited Lumbini in 1952. Returning from a journey to Mustang he descended to the Terai and visited Lumbini, where he saw the Ashoka Pillar and the Nativity Sculpture. He however finds Lumbini in a state of deterioration as he described: 'Stone by stone, brick by brick, all the works erected in his honour have crumbled.' (1977, p. 75)

On the occasion of the Fourth General Conference of the World Fellowship of Buddhists, held in Kathmandu in 1956, delegates expressed the urgent need to restore the Sacred Garden of Lumbini and to develop it in accordance with the historical and religious importance of the place. King Mahendra offered his assistance in providing basic facilities and recreating a Buddhist environment and a *vihara* (monastery), a rest house, roads and other infrastructure were constructed.

In 1962, Debala Mitra, Director-General of the Archaeological Survey of India, visited Lumbini and excavated a small trench to the west of the Ashoka Pillar to determine the nature of the base of the pillar. (Mitra, 1972)

Involvement of the United Nations

The interest and involvement of the United Nations in Lumbini was established through the visit of Secretary-General U Thant in 1967. U Thant believed Lumbini should be a place where religious and secular leaders could work together to create a world free from hunger and strife. Deeply impressed by Lumbini's sanctity, he discussed with the Government of Nepal how best to develop Lumbini into an international pilgrimage and tourism centre. U Thant called upon the international community to come forward to help Lumbini at the UN General Assembly held in Geneva in 1970. The International Committee for the Development of Lumbini was formed in 1970 in New York, under the chairmanship of Nepal's Permanent Representative to the United Nations. This was followed by the United Nations commissioning Japanese Architect Kenzo Tange to prepare the Master Plan for Lumbini, which was finalized and approved by the UN and the Government of Nepal in 1978. (The Kenzo Tange Master Plan is explained in detail in Perception Four of this publication).

In 1997, Lumbini, the birthplace of Lord Buddha was inscribed on the UNESCO List of World Heritage. Following inscription, UNESCO has been involved in supporting the Government of Nepal in monitoring the state of conservation of the World Heritage Property.

Visits and statements by UN Secretary-Generals
(UNESCO 2013)

© UN

Dag Hammarskjöld

Dag Hammarskjöld (Visit March 1959)

Like glittering sunbeams
The flute notes reach the gods
In the birth grotto.
(Haiku from 'A Reader's Guide to Dag Hammarskjöld's Wayward')

© UN

U Thant

U Thant (Visit April 1967)

The visit to Lumbini was 'one of the most important days of my life'. Since early 1968, various phases of development works has been carried out both by the Government of Nepal and by United Nations Organizations and the project have now reached a stage where financing from voluntary contributions will be needed before it can become a pilgrimage centre with adequate facilities for pilgrims and tourists. In this connection I would like also to express my personal appreciation to the Government of Nepal for the initiatives they have already taken. May I also express my sincere hope that both interested governments, individuals and private groups will make generous contributions in cash or kind to help in the implementation of what I consider to be a most worthy project. (Speech during a meeting of the International Committee for the Development of Lumbini, 1970)

Kurt Waldheim (Visit February 1981)

Kurt Waldheim

Through the efforts of the Government of Nepal and with financial assistance from the United Nations Development Programme, a Master Plan has been completed by the Japanese architect Kenzo Tange. However, it is necessary to make these plans a reality. It is my hope, therefore, that government, private institutions and individuals will make generous contributions toward this most worthy undertaking. (Lumbini Development Trust)

Javier Perez de Cuellar (Visit March 1989)

Javier Perez de Cuellar

Buddha's message of compassion and devotion to the service of humanity is more relevant today than at any other time in history. Peace, understanding and a vision that transcends purely national boundaries are imperatives of our insecure nuclear age.
The United Nations is proud to have whole-heartedly supported this project from its inception. I wish to take this further opportunity to state that it will continue to play its parts in support of this undertaking which relates most closely to the spiritual and cultural heritage of humanity. (Speech delivered in Lumbini as reported in The Rising Nepal)

Boutros-Boutros Ghali (November 1993)

Boutros-Boutros Ghali

The implementation of the Lumbini Master Plan is still in progress. I should therefore like to call on the international community, governments, private institutions and individuals to consider contributing to the cause of preserving the tradition of the Buddha — that of compassion and devotion to the service of humanity. (Lumbini Development Trust)

Kofi Annan (December 1998)

Kofi Annan

As the most sacred place of pilgrimage for the world's Buddhists, Lumbini provides yet another illustration of the inter-connectedness of all people, across borders and across time. As a United Nations Educational, Scientific and Cultural Organization (UNESCO) World Heritage Site, Lumbini reminds us how much the world's religions can teach us, Buddhists and non-Buddhists, believers and non-believers alike. And let us applaud the commitment to tolerance that allows a Buddhist summit to be held in an officially Hindu country. The world could use many more such examples of religious harmony. (Message to the first World Buddhist Summit, Lumbini, December 1998)

Ban Ki-Moon (Visit November 2008)

Ban Ki-Moon

I am awestruck by the beauty and profound significance of this site, the birthplace of the Lord Buddha. Being here, I am reminded of his amazing life journey from sheltered prince to founder of one of the world's great religions. And I am moved by his example of voluntarily leaving behind comfortable circumstances to confront the painful realities of life and to help others overcome them. Above all, as Secretary-General of the United Nations, I am all the more inspired to work for peace throughout the world. I sincerely hope that we can learn from his lessons, from his teachings and his philosophy to bring peace, stability, harmony, reconciliation and friendship among people of different beliefs, different religions and cultures. This is exactly what human beings should promote and pursue for a better world, a more peaceful, more prosperous world. (The Rising Nepal)

Perception Three

Re-discovering Lumbini.
Archaeology and site interpretation

The site of Lumbini tells a story that has been unfolding for over 2,500 years. This story can be read by interpreting the evidence that has accumulated over time. Lumbini's archaeological features need to be excavated, analysed and interpreted by a multi-disciplinary team to widen our understanding of the significance and importance of the cultural and natural history of the site.

Content

History of research. Stage 1 – Rediscovery. Stage 2 – Reconstruction. Stage 3 – Conservation. Stage 4 – Re-excavation. Construction periods. Categories of monuments in Lumbini. Period I: Pre-Mauryan period. Period II: Mauryan Period. Period III: Sunga Period. Period IV: Kushan Period. Period V: Gupta Period. Period VI: Medieval Period. Period VII: Modern Period in Lumbini.

References

This chapter is based on the contributions by Robin Coningham with the assistance of Jennifer Tremblay. Reference has also been taken from contributions by Basanta Bidari and Angela Atzori.

History of research

The original search and rediscovery of the natal landscape of the historical Buddha was not a professional or scientific endeavour but representative of archaeology and antiquarian research at the time. Indeed, the development of 'Buddhist' archaeology in the nineteenth century was led by individuals drawn from the civil service and military backgrounds. These antiquarians began to uncover and record temples, monasteries, stupas, pillars and inscriptions from all corners of the sub-continent and at the same time, search for, and translate, surviving texts that shed light on these ancient monuments. Many of these individuals, often referred to as 'orientalists', belonged to the Royal Asiatic Society of Bengal and regularly published articles on the discovery and translation of monuments and texts (Allen, 2002).

Two of the most influential texts to be discovered and translated were the aforementioned accounts of two Chinese pilgrims Faxian (Fa Hsien) in the fourth and fifth centuries CE and Xuanzang (Hiuen Tsiang) in the seventh century CE, who came to South Asia in search of Buddhist scriptures from the natal lands of the Buddha (Coningham, 2001, p. 63).

These topographical accounts of the great monuments and Buddhist kingdoms from Gandhara in the west to Anuradhapura in the south captured the imagination of many individuals, particularly Alexander Cunningham, who dedicated himself in the pursuit of the Buddhist landscape described by Faxian and Xuanzang. Whilst Cunningham was able to identify many key sites from the pilgrims' accounts, including Kushinagar and Bodhgaya, he was unable to locate the birthplace itself. Indeed, the location of Lumbini remained uncertain until 1893 when Jaskaran Singh, an officer serving the Government of Nepal, reported the discovery of an Ashoka Pillar on the bank of a large tank called Nigalihawa Sagar in the Nepal Terai and Anton Führer, archaeological surveyor of the North-western Provinces and Oudh Circle, was sent in 1896 to investigate it (Mitra, 1972, p. 5; Falk, 1998, p. 5).

It is important to realise that since its rediscovery in 1896, Lumbini has experienced significant changes over the past century as each successive excavator, architect and conservator has altered its landscape. This process of conservation and presentation may be divided into four main stages: re-discovery 1896-99; reconstruction 1933-39; conservation 1962-1985; and re-excavation 1992-1997.

Remains of monastries in the Sacred Garden

Stage 1 - Rediscovery

Anton Führer and Khadga Shamsher Rana (1896)

Although there is some debate as to the exact sequence of events, which led to the identification and rediscovery of the site of ancient Lumbini, most scholars accept that during Anton Führer's investigations, he was requested to meet General Khadga Shamsher Rana, the Governor of Palpa, at his camp near the village of Padariya, 21 miles to the south-east (Allen, 2008, p. 134). Padariya lay five miles from the Indian border and had been cleared of jungle a generation earlier, but less than half a mile to the north-east of the village was a 'five acre thicket of trees, breaking the flat level of the surrounding plough-land, bounded by a small meandering stream on its eastern side and a small pond on the south' (Führer, 1972, p. 28). Within this raised thicket, Anton Führer was able to discern four mounds, and on the largest stood a small, box-like temple dedicated to the goddess Rupadevi (Führer, Allen, 2008, p. 135). Anton Führer described it as a 'small modern mean-looking temple, dedicated to that goddess, which was erected by a Saiva ascetic on top of one of the ruined stupas about four years ago' (Führer, 1972, p. 28) Inside the temple, Anton Führer identified the statue of Rupadevi as a partial scene representing Mayadevi giving birth to Sakyamuni Buddha (Allen, 2008, p. 135).

Adjacent to the temple, on the western side of the mound was a broken pillar rising about 10 feet from the ground. The pillar was missing its capital and appeared to have suffered a lightning strike at some point, as it was split down the middle, but there was a visible medieval inscription. Anton Führer and Khadga Shamsher employed their labourers to dig around the base of the pillar and uncovered another inscription, this one in the familiar Brahmi script, often associated with Ashoka (Allen, 2008). The identification of the site of ancient Lumbini was made possible in the first two lines of the inscription initially translated as: 'Beloved of the gods, King Piyadasi (Asoka) when 20 years consecrated came to worship saying here the Buddha was born Sakyamuni (Allen, 2008, p. 139). Although some have attributed the rediscovery of Lumbini to Anton Führer, the site and the pillar were already known, as Khadga Shamsher had sent rubbings of the medieval inscription to Vincent Smith some years earlier, who failed to recognize the importance of the site (Allen, 2008).

With the discovery of Lumbini and the birthplace of Kanakamuni Buddha at Niglihawa Sagar, Anton Führer felt he had all of the clues that he needed to rediscover Kapilavastu, the childhood home of the Sakyamuni Buddha. Using the Chinese pilgrims' accounts, Anton Führer proclaimed that Kapilavastu lay 18 miles north-west of the Lumbini Pillar and six miles north-west of the Nigalihawa Sagar Pillar and henceforth announced his discovery of the famed city of the Shakyas (Allen, 2008, p. 140).

Lumbini ruins viewed from the South, 1899, from the report of P. C. Mukherji

Purna Chandra Mukherji (1899)

Shortly after Anton Führer announced his discovery of Kapilavastu, his work came under close scrutiny and he resigned from his post as Archaeological Surveyor of North Western Provinces and Oudh. In order to investigate the quality of Anton Führer's discoveries, the Government of North Western Provinces and Oudh commissioned Laurence Austine Waddell and Purna Chandra Mukherji to explore the Nepal Terai and plan and excavate the Buddhist sites within it (Allen, 2008, p. 182). Purna Chandra Mukherji was subsequently deputed to plan and excavate Lumbini, Sagarhawa (the site of the Sakya massacre), Kudan and research the location

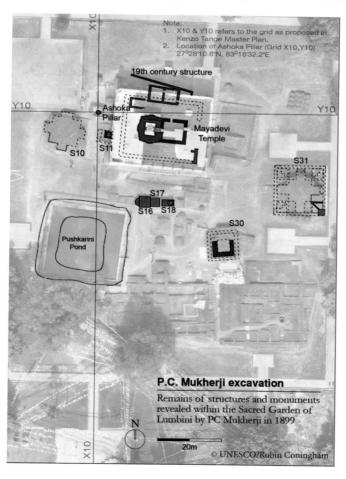

P.C. Mukherji excavation

Remains of structures and monuments revealed within the Sacred Garden of Lumbini by PC Mukherji in 1899

20m

© UNESCO/Robin Coningham

of the long lost city of Kapilavastu at Tilaurakot (Mukherji, 1969). There, Purna Chandra Mukherji and a small group of workers began excavation on the ruined *kot* on the east bank of the Banganga River, which revealed the extensive citadel walls as well as several stupas and *vihara*s (Mukherji, 1969, p. 21).

Purna Chandra Mukherji conducted a brief exploration and excavation in Lumbini in 1899. He excavated the southern side of the Mayadevi Temple and exposed carved brick masonry, of the type found along the western and northern edges. He located seven minor projections on each side, which indicated the temple was known in the Silpashastra, the classical text on architecture, as *Saptaratha*, the 'Seven-bayed Temple'. He successfully interpreted the narrative of the nativity sculpture where Mayadevi is represented holding on to a branch of the ashoka tree at the time of delivery, while other attendants are variously helping her. Below and between them stands the infant Bodhisattva (Mukherji, 1969, pp 34-39).

Whilst working in Lumbini, Purna Chandra Mukherji sketched plans of the standing ruins as well as excavating several trenches around the Ashoka Pillar and the Mayadevi Temple, atop which the small modern temple dedicated to Rupadevi had been erected. Purna Chandra Mukherji's brief report describes it as an 'ancient site [that is] full of ruins. Wherever I excavated, walls of ancient structures were brought to light'. However, Purna Chandra Mukherji's recording and excavating technique reflected the time and he concentrated on describing the Ashokan inscription, the decorative plinth of one phase of the Mayadevi Temple and the Gupta period sculpture of Mayadevi. After Purna Chandra Mukherji's initial excavations in 1899, the site of Lumbini was left relatively untouched until the 1930s, when Keshar Shamsher Rana – a nephew of Khadga Shamsher Rana, who directed Anton Führer to Lumbini – carried out large scale excavations and reconstruction at the site (Mukherji, 1969, pp 34-39).

Between the fifteenth century and the late eighteenth centuries, there is very little evidence of construction on the site, and it is likely that as the site fell into obscurity, the monuments of the past were gradually covered by vegetation. Indeed, when Anton Führer and Khadga Shamsher Rana rediscovered Lumbini in 1896, they found a 'mutilated pillar rising about 10-feet above ground' (Führer, 1972, p.28). As noted above, Anton Führer also described 'a small modern mean-looking building, which was about four years ago erected by a Saiva ascetic on top of one of the ruined stupas'

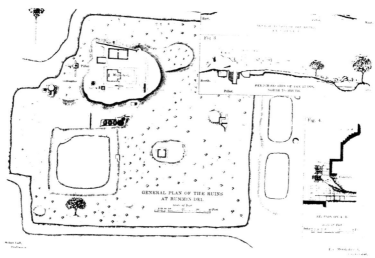

General plan and section of Lumbini, 18899, from the report of P. C. Mukherji

(1972). Presumably the ruined structures he refers to were the remains of the uppermost eroded remains of one of the final phases of the ancient Mayadevi temple. Levels, which were demolished or collapsed, and in the 1890s used as foundations for the new simple, square temple recorded by Purna Chandra Mukherji in a photograph. As noted above, the nativity image was at that time thought to represent a local deity, Rupadevi, and was worshipped as such. A house for the priest was also constructed just north of this temple on the grassy mound that now buried the earlier platform and temple stages. Anton Führer also described four ruined stupas, close to the pillar, the bathing tank, the two fountains and the well mentioned by the two Chinese pilgrims (1972). Unfortunately, Anton Führer did not provide any plans of the site, but it was not long before Purna Chandra Mukherji visited Lumbini in 1899 to conduct brief excavations and plan the site. As noted above, when Purna Chandra Mukherji visited the site it was in a similar condition to that found by Anton Führer and Khadga Shamsher Rana three years previously and the mound was covered with a number of saplings and trees. He recognized and excavated the decorative plinth of the Mayadevi Temple, as well as numerous stupas and structures surrounding it. His actions initiated a new period of development for the site, as he began the process of removing the accumulated debris and sediment burying the garden, uncovering the structures, and creating an artificial landscape, in which centuries of site development and phases of construction are exposed simultaneously to the visitor.

Stage 2 – Reconstruction

Keshar Shamsher Rana (1933 to 1939)

Between 1933 and 1939 General Keshar Shamsher Rana conducted a major excavation of the ruins in Lumbini. Unfortunately, there is little to report concerning these excavations as there is almost no documentation of the nature of his work. However, his work had an enormous impact, which can still be seen today, as he removed metres of the later deposits covering the site. As is clear from photographs taken in the early 1930s, Lumbini was in need of conservation but the techniques and methods utilised involved the destruction of many of the existing structures and the rebuilding of the new temple and complete remodelling of the bathing pool. The backfill from the excavations was formed into two stupa-like mounds to the north and south of the temple. These monuments were later to be confused by pilgrims for Buddhist stupas.

The site was largely left in this state until 1962, when the Archaeological Survey of India (ASI) returned to the Terai to investigate the natal landscape of the Buddha equipped with the new archaeological techniques that had been developed in India over the past six decades (Mitra 1972).

The second phase of modern construction resulted in significant changes in the appearance of the site as Keshar Shamsher Rana rebuilt the Mayadevi temple, altered the Pushkarini Pond and countless other structures. As

Back fill from 1930s excavations forming stupa-like structure, taken in 1969

previously mentioned, Keshar Shamsher Rana's excavations from 1933-39 were unrecorded, but there are a few photographs before the excavations and after that prove that this phase was indeed more of a demolition and reconstruction campaign rather than one of excavation and conservation. All we can be sure of is that Keshar Shamsher Rana demolished a number of the smaller stupas that surrounded the original Mauryan stupa (S-6) and destroyed much of the ornately decorated plinth and brick platform of the Mayadevi Temple that had been built in the Gupta period (Allen, 2008, p. 233). He replaced the Hindu temple of the 1890s with another, set on a modern brick platform. Keshar Shamsher Rana also dug out and re-shaped the Pushkarini Pond into a rectangle with stone steps, similar to a bathing ghat and used the backfill from his excavations to create two new earthen stupa–like mounds to the north and south of the new temple (Allen, 2008). This phase, which we have very little record of, changed not only the site itself, but also significantly its public image. It was no longer an overgrown mound of ruins hidden in the Terai, but a curated site with a single focal point — the temple with a single tree to its west, the other trees and saplings having been removed.

Debala Mitra (1962)

The joint project between the ASI and the Government of Nepal's Department of Archaeology (DoA) was led by the Director of the ASI, Debala Mitra. The project surveyed over thirty sites in the Nepal Terai and carried out excavations at Tilaurakot, Kodan and Lumbini.

Debala Mitra's excavations at Lumbini in 1962 were limited to the western side of the pillar, in order to ascertain the base of the Ashoka Pillar. She noticed that the pillar had a Mauryan polish typical of finished stone from a quarry in the neighbourhood of Chunar (near Varanasi, U.P., India). She wished to reach the base of the pillar in order to determine the length of its unpolished portion, but was unable to do so. She was unable to go beyond 51 cm below the polished portion because concerns had been raised by the Nepali authorities about the stability of the pillar, which already was recorded as tilting. However, she succeeded in preparing an inventory of a number of the key artefacts excavated by Keshar Shamsher Rana in Lumbini.

Debala Mitra's observations of the condition of the site were critical, writing that 'practically nothing has been done to conserve the monuments of Lumbini' (Mitra, 1972, p. 196). She noted that the group of sixteen small votive stupas, which she saw during a visit in 1957, were completely demolished and several of the structures exposed by Mukherji in 1899 could no longer be traced. Debala Mitra also criticized the excavations of Keshar Shamsher Rana stating that the unscientific technique employed had led to the damage and wholesale destruction of many structures (Mitra, 1972, p. 197). Some of the artefacts uncovered during Keshar Shamsher Rana's excavation were found in the home of a Buddhist monk, who was a member of the Lumbini Dharmodaya Committee and lived in the old rest house. However, any further information regarding their original contexts or exact locations had been lost to time (Mitra, 1972). After Mitra's brief work at Lumbini in 1962, the site remained in a largely unchanged state until 1967 when UN Secretary-General U Thant visited Lumbini.

© Bridget Allchin

Sacred Garden with Ashoka Pillar to the right, taken in 1969

Stage 3 - Conservation
Department of Archaeology, Nepal (1972-1985)

The visit of UN Secretary-General U Thant to Lumbini acted as a major catalyst for the development of Lumbini into a tourism and pilgrimage centre. The newly formed Lumbini Development Committee (LDC) engaged the Japanese architect Kenzo Tange to develop a plan which saw the site divided into three distinct areas, linked by walkways and canals. At the southern end of the site, the Sacred Garden was focused on the key archaeological monuments, but was linked to a secular administrative and visitor induction zone to the north through a middle monastic area.

As a result of these major design initiatives, archaeological excavations were restarted by the Department of Archaeology in 1970 and 1971, with the principal aim of locating the Lumbini village, as mentioned in the inscription on the Ashoka Pillar (Bidari, 2004, p. 89) The village, Lumbini Game, was identified around and under the modern police station and the excavations indicated that the earliest habitation probably dated to the sixth century BCE (Bidari, 2004, p. 7) . In parallel, throughout the 1970s and early 1980s, most of the work within the Sacred Garden was focused on restoring existing monuments rather than exposing further structures (Bidari, 2004; Rijal, 1979, p. 90). Indeed, Babu Krishna Rijal reconstructed many of the monuments that were exposed by Keshar Shamsher Rana in the 1930s, particularly around the walls of the temple and the Mauryan stupa (S-6), which had been all but removed by previous excavations.

After conducting excavations almost every year from 1975 to 1983, Babu Krishna Rijal and the LDC were able to establish a cultural sequence for the site, beginning with the period of the Northern Black Polished (NBP) ware (Bidari, 2004, p. 90). In 1984 and 1985, Tara Nanda Mishra conducted additional excavations around the Mayadevi Temple complex, constructing a stratigraphic sequence of six layers beginning with NBP ware and ending with the Khasiya Malla period in the 9th-14th centuries CE. The next stage in the conservation and excavation of Lumbini began in 1990 when the Japanese Buddhist Federation and the newly named Lumbini Development Trust (LDT) proposed a major restoration project at the site (Bidari, 2004).

The next activities at the site were driven by the conservation of the Mayadevi Temple and its surrounding monuments. After U Thant's visit, the next two decades of archaeology were focused on repairing and conserving the site (Figure 15-16). The monuments exposed and repaired by Keshar Shamsher Rana had slowly eroded as the seasonal rains wore away the fragile brickwork and some of the archaeological remains were removed and used by pilgrims and labourers for temporary ovens and new structures. Immediate action was needed to prevent further destruction, and it was during this time that the Master Plan was conceived, designed and started. Thus, the archaeological activities of the 1970s and 1980s were focused on the standing remains as Mishra and Rijal both restored and rebuilt the majority of the structures at the site. Whilst this work helped to secure the structures from further harm, the reconstruction was based on hypothetical interpretations of the buildings based on fragmentary plans. Moreover, much of the conservation was carried out using materials that Rijal and Mishra sourced from new and old spoil heaps, parts of collapsed remains, and accumulated on-site debris. Many of these materials were Mauryan brickbats and, as a result, many monuments at Lumbini have a uniform appearance and it has become difficult to identify or examine the various earlier stages of construction. The first stages of the Master Plan also involved the construction of a levee and water body around the central archaeological site, dividing Lumbini into the planned three zones, thereby changing the way in which the site was accessed and viewed (Weise, 2008, p. 34).

© Song Yan Gang

Ancient brick cross-walls in the Mayadevi Temple

Stage 4 – Re-excavation

Japanese Buddhist Federation (JBF) and UNESCO (1992-1996)

In 1990, the JBF and the LDT agreed to undertake a large scale excavation of the Mayadevi Temple. The primary objective of the joint excavation was the immediate restoration of the temple which was suffering damage from the deep roots of the tree to its immediate west. The work began in 1992 with the dismantling of the modern temple and excavation down to the Mauryan occupation period.

The excavation work, supported by the DoA, continued up to 1996. These excavations revealed that the temple mound comprised the foundations and ruins of a number of different construction periods, the earliest of which utilized burnt bricks and was dated by the excavators to the third century BCE. The most important finding from their excavation is the Marker Stone, which has been interpreted by many scholars as representing the exact birth place of Lord Buddha. Also recovered were a terracotta panel depicting the 'Great Renunciation' of Siddhartha Gautama, terracotta human and animal figurines, beads and bangles, stone objects and punch-marked and other coins. Although preliminary reports were circulated in 2001 and 2005, the full final report of the excavations and its findings remain unpublished.

In 1997, Lumbini was declared a UNESCO World Heritage Property and the next challenge of JBF and LDT was the conservation of the exposed structures. While the JBF wanted to backfill the remains, insisting that this was the only way to truly preserve them, the LDT wanted to display them to the public, and create a permanent structure to house the ruins. (Japanese Buddhist Federation, 2001, p. 13)

The final stage of the modern development of Lumbini involved joint excavations by the JBF and LDT in the 1990s. During this time, the Mayadevi Temple built in the 1930s by Keshar Shamsher Rana was deconstructed one phase at a time until the excavators reached the Mauryan period of brick construction, and this is how the site is seen by visitors today. The team did, however, leave a pillar-shaped bulk of brickwork in the north-west corner of the temple in an attempt to display the phases of structural stratigraphy. The excavators then protected the Mauryan remains by refilling the earliest internal chambers with sand and brick and building a temporary shelter of scaffolding and corrugated iron over all the remains in the temple (Japanese Buddhist Federation, 2001, pp. 91-93).

It had not been decided what to do with the temporary protective structure in the year 2000 when a 'Reactive Monitoring Mission' of Lumbini was dispatched by UNESCO to assess the state of the site. The mission advised that the proposal by the LDT for a new solid structure might damage the remains and would certainly alter the appearance of the Sacred Garden. The mission offered a series of eight criteria to be followed in order to preserve the authenticity of the site, including: non-intrusive; reversibility; shelter; visibility; focus; access; worship; and the use of authentic materials (Coningham and Milou, 2000).

Finally, in 2002, due to damage by high winds and extreme weather conditions, a more permanent steel and brick shelter was built to protect the Mauryan Temple's foundations and the Marker Stone inside the temple was sealed beneath a bulletproof sheet.

The new protective structure

The new closed shelter of steel and brick was completed in 2002 and, as anticipated by earlier technical advisers, it resulted in the creation of an adverse micro-climate within the temple. Increased levels of humidity, exasperated by growing numbers of visitors and pilgrims, began to accelerate biological growth on both the Ashokan brick surfaces and the Marker Stone. Moreover, the fluctuating water-table resulted in the saturated brick walls of the Ashokan Temple becoming subject to damaging salt efflorescence. In reaction to these potentially irreversible developments and other challenges facing the development of an Integrated Management Plan, the Government of Nepal and UNESCO jointly secured funding from Japanese Funds-in-Trust for the Preservation of the World Cultural Heritage for UNESCO in 2010 to address issues of conservation and management at the World Heritage Site. The project was entitled 'Strengthening the Conservation and Management of Lumbini, the Birthplace of Lord Buddha, World Heritage Property' and focused on five main components: the conservation of the Ashoka Pillar, the Marker Stone, the Nativity Sculpture and brick structures; the evaluation, definition and interpretation of the archaeological signature of the site; the finalisation of the KenzoTange Master Plan; the development of an Integrated Management Plan; and capacity building for individuals working at the site. The first two activities necessitated the exposure and study of the Ashokan Temple walls within the modern shelter and three years of scientific investigation and analysis between 2010 and 2013 have shed light on the unique sequence of construction within the Mayadevi Temple and provided the necessary information for its long-term conservation and protection.

Geophysical survey and auger coring

A UNESCO mission was carried out by the University of Bradford in 2001. This environmental and geophysical survey of the site involved magnetometry, resistivity, auger coring, and several months of temperature and humidity observations. The geophysical plots revealed several fairly well defined areas of sub-surface remains and the magnetic signatures of these are indicators of brick rubble and probably demolition before a phase of rebuilding. If this is correct, it again confirms the continuous occupation and restructuring of the Mayadevi Temple site and the artificial nature of the current ground surface of the Sacred Garden. This non-destructive mission was also the first following Rijal's excavations of 1970-71 to investigate the village mound to the south-west of the Sacred Garden complex. The presence of the modern police station on this site caused considerable interference with these results, but the report of this mission did confirm several ephemeral curvilinear features in the area, possibly small enclosures on the edge of the village and a well-defined feature which could represent a brick rubble path. The auger survey was conducted by boring to a maximum depth of 3.5 metres at intervals in transecting oriented north-south and east-west across the Sacred Garden complex, and on a smaller scale over the Village Mound. By measuring the thickness of sediments from these samples, the team established depths for the probable natural soil surface, and were able to construct a theoretical sub-surface profile in two planes across the site.

These profiles, and an analysis of the sediment types showed that the Sacred Garden complex stands on an underlying natural rise of thick clay sediments, which are cut further from the garden by buried channels or pits, probably paleo-channels of the river which currently runs in several stream-beds to the east of the site, but which is known to change course during the regular seasonal flooding of the surrounding area . This buried surface is then covered by a deep stratigraphy of accumulated sediments and surfaces, which is deepest under the temple complex and is representative of the long history of occupation and use of the site. The village mound is likewise apparently an amalgamation of a natural clay rise and accumulated sediments comprised of building remains, debris and occupation surfaces. The logical conclusion, therefore, is that the Sacred Garden and the Village Mound were chosen for occupation because they represented a relative haven from the seasonal flooding of the plains. However, the team also recognized that years of excavation and redistribution of soil and material around the site has left it extremely vulnerable to flooding in its exposed pits, wells and trenches, and this has led to the current need for rescue work and conservation in the Sacred Garden (Coningham and Schmidt 2002; Coningham et al. 2011).

© UNESCO/Nabha Thapa

Archaeological research in 2011

Construction periods

As discussed above, the site of Lumbini has undergone numerous excavations and investigations during the last century, beginning with Purna Chandra Mukherji in 1899 and continuing most recently with JBF and LDT in 1992-1997. Each of these excavations were carried out using different excavation, surveying and recording methods and none of the subsequent reports provide a thorough and comprehensive phasing of the site. Indeed, most of the available reports on the site have failed to date the structures and where estimated dates have been provided, explanations of the methods used, artefacts unearthed, or contexts explored have been patchy or missing. In addition, there is no single accepted system for identification of the structures and very few authors have published maps, sketches, plans or photographs, which makes a re-examination of their findings almost impossible. Finally, the conservation carried out on the site has radically changed the way in which the site is viewed and the reuse of materials such as archaeological brickbats to repair and reconstruct the monuments, which has given them a uniform appearance making it very difficult to date and phase them as they now stand. However, based on the limited data available, it is possible to identify at least seven periods of construction within the site (Bidari, 2004, p. 180):

Period	Name	Date
Period I	Pre-Mauryan	Fourth century BCE
Period II	Mauryan	Third century BCE
Period III	Sunga	Second to first century BCE
Period IV	Kushan	First to second century CE
Period V	Gupta	Third to ninth century CE
Period VI	Medieval	Ninth to fourteenth century CE
Period VII	Modern	Ninteenth to twentieth century CE

During these seven general periods of construction, a number of different structures were built and rebuilt, including stupas, *viharas*, chaityas, wells, tanks and temples. However, there is also no clear criteria for identifying the different types of structures in Lumbini and, as a result, archaeologists have labelled them differently. For example, Rijal describes several structures as chaityas, which can mean any structure that marks a sacred spot, such as a stupa, griha or shrine.

Categories of monuments in Lumbini

In a publication by Basanta Bidari in 2002, a plan of the site was provided in which the monuments of the site were labelled. This plan separates structures into stupas, monasteries (*viharas*), and buildings, and assigns each structure a number. For the purposes of this publication, we will adopt these assignments. This helps us avoid the problems raised by previous studies, such as those by Rijal, Mishra and the JBF, which described monument size, shape, decoration, orientation, and distance and direction of one from another. The problem being that as new structures have also been uncovered, reconstructed, or even created on a regular basis on site, the earlier descriptions are unhelpful and the confusion caused by this has meant that the history of several stupas is now in question because it is not clear which structure is being described. Furthermore, the fact that none of the excavation reports have provided a complete record of finds, contexts, site plans, or even an explanation of all work carried out has not helped this matter. Finally, differences in definitions of the types of structures has lead to the situation that it is sometimes unclear precisely what the excavator believes the described monument to be, or how this compares with previous authors' explanations. Rijal, for example, describes many monuments as chaityas, whereas Mishra labels them as temples. To avoid such confusion, a brief outline of the types of structures at Lumbini, and a definition of the terms as used hereafter.

Viharas

*Vihara*s, or monasteries, are the living and meditation places of monks and nuns and are usually organized as a group of cells or rooms surrounding a central courtyard. Mitra first mentioned the *vihara* at Lumbini in 1962, when she discovered a quadrangular brick monastery with an array of cells on four sides near the south-east corner of the bathing pool (1972, p. 197). The same structure was fully uncovered by Mishra in the 1980s and subsequently three other *vihara*s were discovered in the same area, with various phases of construction dating from the Mauryan period to the Gupta period.

Stupas

A stupa is the most distinct and resilient of Buddhist monuments and can be defined as a mound of brick, stone or earth that enshrines a relic or marks a sacred place. (Coningham, 2001, p. 72; Bidari, 2002, p. 101) There are typically four different categories of stupas – those containing the corporeal relics of the Buddha (*saririka*), his disciples and saints; those containing objects of use, such as the Buddha's begging bowl (*paribhogika*); those commemorating incidents from the Buddha's life or places visited by him (*uddesika*) and finally votive stupas, which are built by pilgrims and monks as a way of obtaining merit. (Coningham, 2001, p. 72) In Lumbini there are numerous stupas, which have been built from the Mauryan period onwards to the modern period. Most of the monuments appear to have been votive, built by pilgrims and monks for centuries; although one stupa (S-6) has been identified as belonging to the first category of *saririka* stupas and this will be discussed in greater detail below (Rijal, 1979). As stupas are very distinct structures from the other monuments in Lumbini, there has been relatively little confusion regarding their identification over the years. However, it is worth noting that a stupa can also be referred to as a chaitya, as this term may simply mean 'shrine'.

Chaityas

Although many of those working in Lumbini have made references to the presence of chaityas, the application of this last category of Buddhist monuments is complex as a chaitya may refer to a sacred place, sometimes associated with a relic or event. Indeed, some scholars have referred to a stupa as a chaitya but have also called a temple a chaitya as well. For example, the shrine, which was built over the Marker Stone in the second period of construction of the Mayadevi Temple, has been described by some scholars as a chaitya, but so has the temple itself. Within the varied excavation reports from Lumbini, chaitya seems to have become a catch-all word for any monument that has not been identified as a stupa or *vihara*.

Wells

A number of wells were excavated at both the village site and within the Sacred Garden. Unfortunately, there is almost no information available on the excavations at the village mound, but Rijal does mention the presence of a terracotta ring-well in the earliest phases of the site, as well as a Kushan period well close to the modern LDT Nursery. In 1993, when the water of the Sacred Pond was drained, two artesian wells were discovered in the north-east and south-east corners of the pond. Unfortunately, no additional detailed information was provided on this discovery, but it has been suggested that this may be indicative of Lumbini's role as a waypoint in the ancient trade routes which passed through the Terai (Bidari, 2004, p. 111).

Period I: Pre-Mauryan period

Note:
1. X10 & Y10 refers to the grid as proposed in Kenzo Tange Master Plan.
2. Location of Ashoka Pillar (Grid X10,Y10) 27°28'10.8"N, 83°16'32.2"E

Pre-Mauryan structure

Pre-Mauryan remains revealed from recent excavation

Pushkarini Pond

Pre-Mauryan remains revealed from recent excavation

Pre-Mauryan period

Remains of structures and monuments within the Sacred Garden of Lumbini

N

20m   © UNESCO/Robin Coningham

Pre-Mauryan period phase 1: New investigations carried out by Durham University, the LDT and DOA from 2011 to 2013 within the Sacred Garden and the Mayadevi Temple have greatly advanced knowledge of Pre-Mauryan Lumbini, which has now extended occupation within the vicinity of the site back to the late Chalcolithic period c. 1300 BCE. This earliest evidence was derived from excavations at the Lumbini Village Mound, where trenches were opened at the side of the newly cut levee and on the top of the mound within the police station parade ground next to the Rana rest house. The latter, a 4.5 metre deep trench, yielded evidence of human habitation at the site between 1300 BCE and sixth century CE. The earliest occupation corroborates the early dates of occupation in the vicinity of the stupa at Gotihawa near Tilaurakot and suggests that the Terai had already been settled by sedentary agricultural communities by the beginning of the first millennium BCE. The archaeological sequence of the Village Mound suggests that it was a settlement site with evidence of house floors, metal-working and domestic waste. The low clay mound, on which the settlement was established, rose above the flood plain and research has identified the presence of a silted river channel dating to this time running to the north-west of the Mayadevi Temple complex. There is no evidence of settlement in the vicinity of the temple at this time, but soil micromorphology has identified that this area was under cultivation perhaps by villagers from the ancient Village Mound.

Pre-Mauryan period phase 2: Whilst occupation at the Village Mound was to continue until the sixth century CE, soil micromorphology analysis from within the lowest levels of the trenches cut under the Mayadevi Temple suggested that a low mound was raised in its vicinity by depositing alluvial soil. The first evidence of structural activity at the Mayadevi Temple occurred in the middle of the sixth century BCE with the cutting of a straight line of post holes defining the centre of the mound. Soil micromorphology indicates that the central area of the temple, defined by wooden fence or railing, was void of structures and the stratigraphy and soil sections suggest the presence of substantial roots, perhaps indicative of a tree.

Finds of broken vessels and charcoal outside the fence line, suggest that activities were defined by this first creation of sacred space. This open space at the heart of the Mayadevi Temple appears to have remained a feature of the structure until a major remodelling of the site in the Sunga Period (Phase 2), when this previously open space was sealed below a new brick feature.

Pre-Mauryan period phase 3: The wooden railing surrounding the centre of the Temple Mound was later replaced, or rather reproduced in a more permanent form, through the construction of a double kerb of brick on edge. Tempered with rice husk, these bricks were highly distinctive as they measured 49 × 36 × 7 cm, weighed 20 kg each and had one face marked by deep finger grooves. The area to the immediate south of the kerb was paved with the same bricks, although many of them were broken in antiquity. Surviving areas of this simple brick platform have been identified in other areas of the temple, suggesting that it originally covered an area of some 26 metres north-south and 21 metres east-west. Soil micromorphology indicates that the central area of the temple, now defined by the kerb, continued to be void of brick structures. There is evidence of repair in some parts of the temple with three superimposed layers of paving and also another area of rammed mud floor which included large fragments of brick. Some fragments of wall plaster were also recovered from within the structure during this later repair. This indicates that this material belonged to the earlier phase of temple construction. At the end of its lifespan, the early brick platform temple was enshrined within the brick Ashokan Temple and sealed below the new construction.

© Kai Weise

Pre-Mauryan archaeology within the Mayadevi Temple

Period II: Mauryan Period

The Mauryan, or rather Ashokan, period marks a significant phase in the development of Lumbini. While the site is thought already to have been a place of early pilgrimage, the visit of Ashoka in 249 BCE started the first major period of construction. During this period, a *vihara*, the Ashoka Pillar, the first two phases of the Mayadevi temple and numerous stupas were erected. The *vihara* (V-2) was excavated by Mishra in the 1980s and is located to the south of the Mayadevi Temple, with individual cells on all four sides and a meeting hall in the centre. (Mishra, 1996, pp. 40-41) Unfortunately, there was no mention in the report of how the structure was dated, nor any plans or photographs of the excavations. During his earlier excavations in the 1970s, Rijal described how two stupas to the north of the Mayadevi Temple (S-3 and S4) were datable to the Mauryan period, but again, no justification for this dating process was provided in his report. He also identified another Mauryan stupa with a square foundation five feet north of the Temple (S-6), which had been cut down from the top by three feet, most likely during the excavations carried out by Keshar Shamsher Rana in the 1930s. The base of the stupa contained the lid of a cylindrical gold casket in association with some charred human bones and other ritual offerings – most likely also disturbed in the 1930s (Rijal, 1979). Mishra, in his 1996 report, also mentioned a further two plain rectangular stupas belonging to the Mauryan period, one 35 feet north of the Mayadevi Temple and the other inside a big square stupa. It is unclear, which structure he was referring to 35 feet north of the temple, as none of the plans at the time depicted a stupa at this location, but the large square stupa might be located south of the Mayadevi Temple and possibly identified in Bidari's plan (S-30).

Perhaps the most famous monument in Lumbini, the Ashoka Pillar, provides concrete evidence of the Mauryan presence at the site. The pillar is made of polished Chunar sandstone, weighs 37 tons and stood at a height of 30 feet and 10.5 inches, of which 13 feet and 8.5 inches is buried underground. The pillar is a truncated cone, which tapers from 2 feet and 7.25 inches at the base to 2 feet and 2.5 inches at the top. Mishra

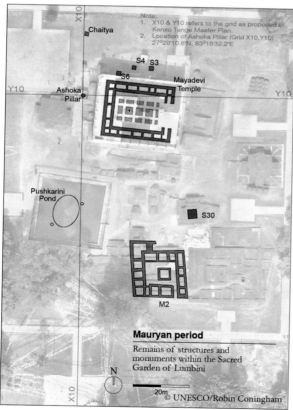

reported that the bottom of the pillar was inserted into the centre of the base slab, with a brick foundation underneath (Bidari, 2004). The pillar visibly tilts and has suffered some damage as a vertical fissure runs down to the middle. The top of the pillar is broken and there is no trace of the horse capital as described by Chinese traveller Xuanzang but part of the base of the capital survives (Mitra, 1972, p. 197). The Ashokan inscription on the pillar is in Brahmi script and has been translated:

> By King Piyadasi, the beloved of the gods [who] having been consecrated twenty years [having] come himself personally [here] to offer homage, or celebrate, because Sakyamuni Buddha was born here, was caused both a Silavigadabhica to be built and a stone pillar to be set up. [And], because the Lord was born here, the Lumbini village was made free from taxes and liable to pay [only] one-eighth part [of the produce]. (Japanese Buddhist Federation, 2001, p. 75)

The only other structure that has been dated to the Mauryan period is that of the Mayadevi Temple. According to the JBF excavations in the 1990s, the first period of construction of the temple can be dated to the Mauryan period and appears to have had at least two phases, referred to as the lower and upper structures, and hereafter as Phase 1 and Phase 2. This period of construction was dated by brick design, the radio-carbon dating of a single charcoal fragment, and small artefacts found in construction contexts, such as two types of NBP ware, grey coloured pottery, red coloured pottery, a marked coin and a copper coin (Japanese Buddhist Federation, 2001, p. 55; 2005, pp. 149-161).

Ashokan Mayadevi Temple phase 1: The earliest phase of the brick-built temple was a double walled structure, with an external pavement and internal floor of brick and nine internal 'chambers'. These chambers were square or rectangular brick-lined pits, approximately 1.5 metres deep, and arrayed in three rows of three. It appears that eight of the pits were filled almost to the top in Phase 1 with rammed earth, and the ninth, referred to by the JBF excavation team as Chamber Two, was filled with bricks. A conglomerate stone of the Siwalik variety (Japanese Buddhist Federation, 2005) was cemented in the top layer of bricks and has been interpreted as marking the actual birthplace of Lord Buddha (Japanese Buddhist Federation, 2001, p. 38). Both the inner and outer walls surrounding the temple have foundation cuttings, with crushed bricks at the base to create a footing for construction. A single course of bricks was laid in a herringbone pattern to create the pavement found on the north and west sides of the temple and a similar pattern of brick-laying created a floor between the double walls and inside the temple.

Ashokan Mayadevi Temple phase 2: Shortly after the construction of Phase 1, there appears to have been a period of reconstruction. This phase more or less followed the ground plan of Phase 1, and used almost identical bricks. It is not known why this rebuilding took place, but the Japanese excavators suggested that it was due to instability in the structural design, or to counter against the regular seasonal flooding of the area. A further six 'chambers' were defined, three to the east and three to the west of the original nine. This brought the total number to fifteen chambers. The floor of the temple itself was then also raised by several courses of bricks and the pits filled accordingly, though again, it is thought that this fill did not quite reach the floor level of the temple. Chamber Two was again filled up with brick, burying the Marker Stone, whereas the remaining chambers were filled with fill (Japanese Buddhist Federation, 2001). The walls were built up from a surviving twelve or thirteen courses of bricks extant from Phase 1 and are narrower than the earlier structures, so that the lower part of the walls project in plan by approximately 20-30 cm compared to the upper Phase 2 courses. A series of support sections were also loosely built between the outer and inner walls at this time, to shore up and stabilize the structure of the inner wall. These support sections are, in most cases, separated from the brick floor between the double walls by a layer of earth, presumed to be a natural build up within the space, rather than an intended foundation.

During the course of the investigations between 2010 and 2013, a number of the old sections left by the JBF team were cleaned and recorded. In particular, this has resulted in the generation of additional information as to the morphology and phasing of the Ashokan period Temple. For example, we now know that the second phase of Ashokan brickwork was associated with the presence of broken ceramic roof tiles in the outermost west, south-west and south-east portions of the temple. The absence of any tile fragments in the central areas in particular, suggests that only the outer edges of the temple were roofed and that the central portion was open to the elements. This hypothesis has been supported by the examination of soil micro-morphology, which has yielded evidence of large roots in antiquity. In addition, more evidence of wall plaster has been recorded from most parts of the second phase of the Ashokan Temple, some of which appears to have been painted.

Period III: Sunga Period

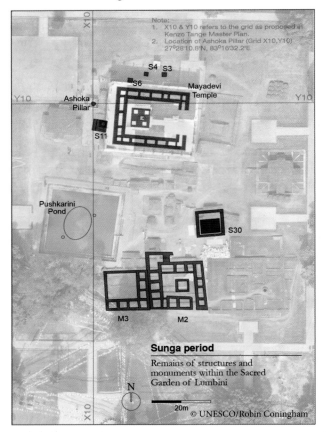

There is some evidence of a Sunga period of construction at the site, although it has not been as readily identified as some of the other phases of development. Monuments attributed by scholars to this period include a *vihara* (V-3) to the west of the Mauryan *vihara* (V-2), the expansion of the big square Mauryan stupa mentioned by Mishra (S-30) and a new period of construction at the Mayadevi Temple. The *vihara* was described by Mishra in his report on the excavations of 1984 and 1985, in which he merely mentions that the only Sunga phase of the structure that could be found are the outer walls, as the rest of it was badly damaged by later periods of construction (1996, p. 41). The Sunga phase of construction on the big square Mauryan stupa, also identified by Mishra, comprises the building of a thick wall around the original stupa and a second wall built five feet from it to create a processional path (Mistra, 1996, p. 42). The JBF noted two distinct periods of construction of the Mayadevi Temple following the Mauryan period, but did not provide any dating evidence for Stage II, and given the nature of the construction carried out, it seems more likely that these were two phases of the same period. However, no material was recovered from the remains that would assist in dating the relevant activities, thus assignment to the Sunga period is not conclusive.

Sunga Mayadevi Temple phase 1: The Japanese excavators have suggested that an exploratory pit was dug into the brick fill of Chamber Two in the temple during this phase in order to confirm the position of the Marker Stone buried by the Period I, Phase 2 construction work. This new pit was then again brick-lined and refilled with earth and broken bricks, and the top was sealed with four large pieces of sandstone, creating a new marker and focus for the temple (Japanese Buddhist Federation, 2001).

Sunga Mayadevi Temple phase 2: A large brick structure was then erected over the Marker Stone, possibly in the form of a stupa. This structure was square, measuring approximately seven metres wide on each face and stood about two metres high. Built into this structure were five chambers – four positioned inside the corners and one central chamber aligned over the sandstone marker. The construction was then capped, but it is not known whether this cap was a plain flat platform or decorated with further structures (Japanese Buddhist Federation, 2001).

Period IV: Kushan Period

The available data for the Kushan period construction at Lumbini is considerably clearer than the Sunga and during this period, several stupas and both existing *vihara*s were rebuilt and enlarged, and a new *vihara* was constructed to the east. The Mayadevi Temple also underwent a further stage of construction and it has been argued that a new well was created in the Nursery Complex of the Lumbini village site. The new *vihara* (V-1) was constructed to the east of the existing *vihara*s and appears to have been rectangular in shape as opposed to the existing square structures. Mishra describes the structure as having living rooms for the monks on three sides – to the north, south and east – as well as a meeting hall on the north side. Again, Mishra did not provide evidence for the dating, or any plans or photographs. He did, however, mention that there are

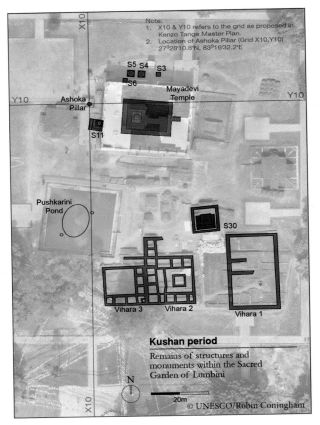

Note:
1. X10 & Y10 refers to the grid as proposed in Kenzo Tange Master Plan.
2. Location of Ashoka Pillar (Grid X10,Y10) 27°28'10.8"N, 83°16'32.2"E

Kushan period

Remains of structures and monuments within the Sacred Garden of Lumbini

N

20m

© UNESCO/Robin Coningham

two brick stupas – one square and the other circular – and a well built of wedge-shaped bricks in the courtyard of the *vihar*. Mishra also mentions the reconstruction of the existing Mauryan *vihara* (V-2), which now had fourteen living rooms on the west, north and south directions, and on the western side there was a veranda towards the courtyard on the east. Mishra identified further construction work during the Kushan phase of the Sunga *vihara*, including a long drain starting from a room on the east and running through the central area, before turning southwards for disposal outside the walls, making a rough 'L' shape in plan. He also mentioned that there were two small water storage tanks in the south-east room of the structure and that the rooms may have been used as a kitchen. One Kushan copper coin was also found in one of the south rooms. With only sketch plans to accompany this phasing, it is difficult to identify exactly, which parts of the structures Mishra is referring to, but it is possible to trace a rectangular structure that is built over both the Sunga and Mauryan *viharas* (V-2 and V-3), which may represent this phase (Mistra, 1996).

Several stupas to the north of the Mayadevi Temple were enlarged during this period with the encasing of earlier rectangular structures within new circular domed stupas. (Rijal, 1979, p. 9) The brick well discovered at the nursery complex of the village site was associated with various animal and bird figurines, and was dated stylistically by these to the Kushan period. The well was built of twentynine courses of solid concave bricks and the bottom level contained some Kushan period spouted pots and a faceted jar. The final period also saw a further redevelopment of the Mayadevi Temple, which the JBF report refers to as Stages 4, 5 and 6. However, based on the structural design of these stages, it seems likely that they were actually three phases of construction in a single stylistic period, and so they are described here together as belonging to Period IV (Rijal, 1996).

Kushan Mayadevi Temple phase 1: This phase saw a new period of major construction work as a large brick and earth platform was created to surround the square brick structure of Phase 2 of the Sunga Period. The containing wall of this platform has not survived fully but the upper surface of this platform was more or less level with the top of the Period II and cut by a series of drains.

Kushan Mayadevi Temple phase 2: A new containing wall of fine clay bricks was built around the platform, which cut off and sealed the ends of the Phase 1 drainage trenches. A hardened surface of earth and traces of plaster sealed the fill of the platform and well packed rows of bricks lining the edges of the platform may have served as a pavement or floor surface. A new entrance stair, decorated with plaster, was built in the middle of the eastern wall and led up to this brick surface.

Kushan Mayadevi Temple phase 3: A new, smaller platform was then built onto this floor level and a small square structure created on top of it, directly over the central chamber of Period II, and therefore the Marker Stone of the Mauryan Period. The base platform of this phase measured 3.1 by 4 metres and was paved with brick and surkhi (a type of mortar). The small square structure above was also constructed in brick and measured around 1.5 by 1.3 metres wide, and around 45 cm high.

Period V: Gupta Period

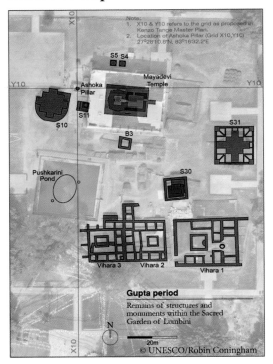

Gupta period

Remains of structures and monuments within the Sacred Garden of Lumbini

20m

© UNESCO/Robin Coningham

The Gupta period of construction at the site is quite distinct as new architectural styles were employed in the building of stupas, *viharas*, temples and the Mayadevi Temple. Mishra describes the stupas built during the Gupta period as having two shapes — square stupas with niche projections on all four sides and steeped rectangular stupas with a flat top. Some of the square structures had a line of tapered and projected bricks separating the lower area with the dome and in one stupa there were a pair of flowers incised on all four corners. Mishra also mentioned that nineteen terracotta seals with Gupta characters were found at a square Gupta-period stupa, however, he did not give any indication as to which structure he was referring to. The only specific stupa that Mishra referred to as having a Gupta construction phase is that of the large square Mauryan stupa (S-30) that was previously renovated in the Sunga period. The Gupta period added walls on all four sides in the square basement. Based on Mishra's description of Gupta period stupas on the site, it is possible to identify several other structures that may have been built or enlarged during this period. An additional period of construction work on the *viharas* has also been noted, in which the orientation of the Kushan period structure (V-1) was changed altogether from a north-south to an east-west alignment. In addition, Mishra mentioned that the *vihara* on the far west, V-3, was also rebuilt in the Gupta period to provide a total of eleven rooms on the east, north and south sides of the building with an *aposthagarasala*, or meeting hall, in the centre. Mishra noted, only briefly, of his discovery of the basements of two Gupta temples (B-3) on the south side of the Mayadevi Temple, but he did not provide further details concerning them. The fifth period of construction at the Mayadevi Temple, which is also thought to have occurred in this period, was characterised by the introduction of an entirely new style and plan of temple, on top of the platform already created (Mishra, 1996).

Gupta Mayadevi Temple phase 1: The first phase of this period saw the construction of a new surface around the square structure built during Phase 3 of the Kushan Period. The new surface brought the surface level of the entire upper platform to the same height as the square structure in its centre.

Gupta Mayadevi Temple phase 2: A small temple was then constructed on top of this platform in highly decorated carved bricks. The building was described by Purna Chandra Mukherji as a seven-bayed *saptaratha* on the basis of its external shape. The plan provided two cells, referred to as a chancel and an ante-chamber. The floor of the chancel was directly above the base platform of the square structure built during Phase 3 of the Kushan Period and followed the same measurements and plan. The excavators have thus argued that a key vertical line was, therefore, maintained throughout all the construction phases of the temple, between the marker stone of the Mauryan Period, and through a series of brick structures which must have held a votive and sacred meaning. The well-known nativity image of the birth of Lord Buddha was also mounted in the chancel, set into the floor just away from the west wall. A flight of six steps led up east out of the chancel to the antechamber and two exits from this room led north and east to the platform and staircase that leads back to the ground level. Whether the level of the antechamber was deliberately raised above the level of the chancel floor to further delimit the sacred space, or whether this was a development of further phases of construction has not been identified in the reports.

Period VI: Medieval Period

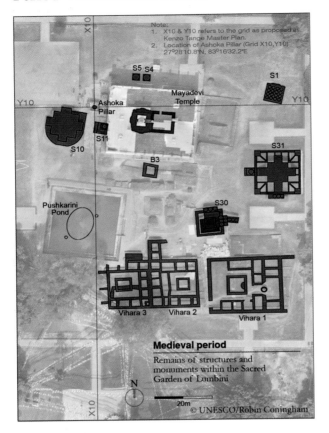

Very little has been written about this period in Lumbini as previous excavations at the village site have only revealed occupation layers dating up to the Gupta period. There is evidence indicating that Lumbini remained a site of pilgrimage well into the medieval period as suggested by the presence of an inscription on the Ashoka Pillar and a number of stupas built on top of existing structures.

The inscription on the pillar is above the Ashoka Pillar inscription and marks the visit of Ripu Malla in the fourteenth century. Ripu Malla was a Prince of the Nagaraja dynasty of western Nepal, who visited the site in 1312 C.E. The inscription consists of a few phrases of a Mahayana Buddhist prayer and the words 'Prince Ripu Malla be victorious'. The inscription has been used as evidence to support the theory that Lumbini and Kapilavastu were widely known to be the birthplace and homeland of Lord Buddha during the medieval period (Mahabodhi Society, 2000).

It was also during this period that a number of votive stupas were erected across the site and Bidari claims that the sixteen votive stupas east of the Mayadevi Temple (S-16), first mentioned by Mitra in 1962, were constructed sometime between the visits of the Chinese travellers in the seventh century and Ripu Malla's visit in the fourteenth century (Bidari, 2002, p. 80). Mishra also describes a series of small votive stupas that were erected during this period on top of the big square stupa (S-30), of which only nine still survive (Mishra, 1996, p. 42).

© Durham University/Mark Household

Scared Garden with pond and Mayadevi Temple in 2012

Period VII: Modern Period in Lumbini

Note:
1. X10 & Y10 refers to the grid as proposed in Kenzo Tange Master Plan.
2. Location of Ashoka Pillar (Grid X10,Y10) 27°28'10.8"N, 83°16'32.2"E

Archaeological revelations until 1969

Remains of structures and monuments revealed within the Sacred Garden of Lumbini by 1969

20m © UNESCO/Robin Coningham

The final period of construction and deposition in Lumbini occurred in the modern period, between the rediscovery of the site in 1896 and the present day. Indeed, the site has experienced significant changes over the past century as each excavation has changed the landscape in numerous ways. As discussed previously, this final period may be divided into four distinct phases: re-discovery (1896-99); reconstruction (1933-39); conservation (1962-1985); and re-excavation (1992-1997).

© Kai Weise

Vessel found in ancient Lumbini Village mound and bowl found in ancient monastery area in 2012

Perception Four

Tranquillity, universality, clarity. The Kenzo Tange Master Plan

When U Thant, Secretary-General of the United Nations from 1961 to 1971, visited Lumbini in 1967, he initiated a campaign to develop the sacred place. Various experts visited the site and prepared the basis for an elaborate plan. The Master Plan that was prepared by Kenzo Tange between 1972 and 1978 defines an area of five by five miles. At the centre of this lies the Sacred Garden. The plan presents the concept for the Sacred Garden, which covers an area of 1,600 by 1,360 metres. A water body and levee defines an inner garden with the main archaeological site around the Ashoka Pillar and an outer area left as a natural forest.

Content

United Nations' role. Allchin-Matsushita report (1969). UN brochure on Lumbini - 'The birthplace of Buddha' (1970). UN Lumbini Development Project Report of the Advisory Panel (1971). Final outline design for Lumbini (1972). Master Design for the Development of Lumbini (1976-1981). Conceptual elements of the Kenzo Tange Master Plan. Sacred Garden as per the Master Plan. Architectural Design for the Lumbini Garden. Major changes during planning phase (1969 to 1981).

References

This chapter is based on contributions by Yukio Nishimura, Takefumi Kurose and Ruprama Rai. References are also attributed to Basanta Bidari.

United Nations' role

The pilgrimage of the then Secretary-General of the United Nations, U Thant, to Lumbini in April 1967 became a landmark in the history of the development of Lumbini. U Thant, believed Lumbini should be a place where religious and secular leaders could work together to create a world free from hunger and strife. Deeply impressed by Lumbini's sanctity, he discussed with the Government of Nepal how best to develop Lumbini into an international pilgrimage and tourism centre.

Subsequent to U Thant's visit, a mission was carried out between April and May 1968 by John Pollaco for UNESCO and a report was prepared the following year. A further mission was carried out in April 1969 by the Resident Representative of the UN in Kathmandu, Yacoub Joury, who submitted a comprehensive report on the development of Lumbini. This led to a mission by two consultants chosen by UNDP in December 1969: Frank Raymond Allchin and Kazuyuki Matsushita. They prepared a report 'United Nations Lumbini Development Project Report of the Advisory Panel'.

During the tenth session of the General Assembly of the United Nations in Geneva in 1970, U Thant called upon the international community to come forward to help develop Lumbini. In 1970, the International Committee for the Development of Lumbini (ICDL) was formed in New York, under the chairmanship of the Permanent Representative of Nepal to the United Nations. The ICDL initially included thirteen member states, namely, Afghanistan, Myanmar, Cambodia, India, Indonesia, Japan, Laos, Malaysia, Nepal, Pakistan, Singapore, Sri Lanka and Thailand. Later, Bangladesh, Bhutan and the Republic of Korea were included.

In 1970, a brochure was prepared for an appeal by the Secretary-General for coordinated bilateral assistance for the development of Lumbini. This was followed by the Report of the ICDL Advisory Panel in August 1971.

In 1972, the Japanese architect and urban planner Kenzo Tange was awarded the consultancy for the preparation of the Master Plan for the development of Lumbini by the United Nations. In July 1972, the 'Final Outline Design for Lumbini (Phase I)' was prepared. This was followed by the 'Master Design for the Development of Lumbini Phase II, Stage

I Report' in 1976 and Stage II Report in 1977. In 1978, the Master Plan of Lumbini was finalized and approved by the ICDL and Government of Nepal. In the meantime, the Government of Nepal became directly involved through the Lumbini Development Committee in planning the development of Lumbini. The committee acquired 770 hectares of land, relocated villages in the project area, provided basic infrastructure, such as roads, electricity, drinking water, etc., and undertook forestation.

Further work continued on the detailing, which led to preparation of the 'Architectural Design for the Lumbini Garden Phase III, Stage II, Technical Report' and the draft report on the 'Master Design for the Lumbini Garden' in 1981.

Central canal, taken in 2012

Allchin-Matsushita report (1969)

UNDP chose two consultants to begin work on the Lumbini Development Project. The two consultants were Frank Raymond Allchin, lecturer on Indian Studies at Cambridge University, England, and Kazuyuki Matsushita, architect and planner with the firm Tange and Urtec, Tokyo. The mission was carried out during 13 - 25 December 1969 and a report on the Lumbini Development Project was prepared. Although Kenzo Tange did not participate in the mission, he was consulted on the project in Tokyo from this early stage. The consultants were also asked to collect data to be used to prepare a brochure for an appeal by the UN Secretary-General to all nations, especially Buddhist countries for coordinated bilateral assistance for the development of Lumbini. The consultants were also expected to provide some illustrative materials to provide a visual concept of the area.

The report and concept design prepared by Allchin and Matsushita were based on some basic aspects that had been determined in advance. This included that 'the principle location of the activities will be the three square-miles area,' which was to become the site 'for the development of a Sacred Garden and a Pilgrim Village, as well as a Buffer-Zone'.

The consultants were also required to 'explore the access roads to the proposed site with particular emphasis on the Bhairahawa-Lumbini stretch'.

The Allchin-Matsushita Report provided the basis for all further work that went into the Master Plan for Lumbini. A section on the historical

Perception from Allchin-Matsushita report, 1969

© Bridget Allen

Sacred Garden area, taken in 1969

and archaeological context of Lumbini leds to the basic concepts for the Master Plan. The report further provided data relating to specific aspects such as climatic conditions, health, population, arboriculture, agriculture, water supply, electric supply and construction materials. It was clearly indicated that the available data was not sufficient.

The conclusion touched upon the means for choosing the architect or planner. Here the suggestion was not to go for a design competition but to select a 'principle architect of high reputation'. The conclusion further provided suggestions on implementation, organization and maintenance, tourism and further research that are needed.

The report began with a short explanation of the scope and approach of the project and the context. It made a clear recommendation for the complete excavation of the Sacred Garden area before construction or landscaping could begin. It also clearly noted that large areas around the Sacred Garden 'are liable to water logging and even inundation during the monsoon'. Finally, it proposed to build a 'monastic area adjoining the Sacred Garden and remote from the pilgrim village'.

The physical context of Lumbini was described as a flat, featureless region about two miles from the first foothills of the Himalayas, with the view of the hills and the mountains often obscured by the weather. Even the sal forests had already receded northwards with the surrounding countryside comprising mainly of farmland. The villages with the mud houses with thatched roofs and cow dung plastered floors seemed to have changed little over the past 2,500 years.

The report laid down the basic concept for the Master Plan.

> The project for the development of Lumbini offers a remarkable subject and an extremely difficult challenge for the architect and landscape architect. It would seem essential that any work should serve to express the historical and cultural aspect of the site, viewed from the twentieth century, in the light of the universality of the Buddha's message, for the comfort of all people, for the welfare of all people. It should serve to express the early life of the Buddha, and the experiences which paved the way to his Great Renunciation. It should also produce as one of its parts the Pilgrim Village which properly planned will become a centre for local development of all kinds, thus providing a link between the sacred site and the surrounding population. (Allchin and Matsushita, 1969, p. 11)

The report indicated five main elements of the Master Plan.

> The access road (Lumbini Bhairahawa Highway), the Sacred Garden, the monastic enclave adjoining it, the agricultural buffer zones, and the Pilgrim Village'. It further states that 'the main elements of the design must be welded together by a strong and clear-cut conception of the project as a whole. Within the project there must be however, a sense of priority and a well-planned phasing so that the later stages can reflect also the needs discovered during the earlier [planning stage]. To provide the necessary land for the project, H.M's Government Department of Housing and Physical Planning create[d] a controlled area of these one by three miles, having the present garden in its southern section. (Allchin and Matsushita, 1969, p. 11)

The concepts for different components were described.

> The exact alignment of the access road, where it passes through the controlled area, should be left for determination when the Master Plan is drawn up. The overall functions and layout are conceptually defined. The sacred garden will be situated at the southern extremity of the controlled area and the Pilgrim Village will lie to the north of the proposed road from Bhairahawa. There will thus be a distance of about a mile between them. This area will primarily be included in the buffer zones. Across it and linking the other two will be the principle access route to the sacred garden. Within this zone, and adjoining the northern side of the garden, we have inserted an area for the construction

of shrines and monasteries. (Allchin and Matsushita, 1969, p. 13)

In respect to the buffer zones, the report suggested that they may be in part retained for normal agricultural purposes and in part specially planted with trees to provide shelter and wind protection. The report also mentions that: 'As the present day villages provide, even now a close mirror of the life of the Buddha's time we would like to see one or more carefully preserved as 'open air museums' for the observation of visitors'. (Allchin and Matsushita, 1969, p. 14)

The Sacred Garden is specifically described.

At present an area of some 30-acres around the Ashoka Pillar is fenced to from the Lumbini Garden. The whole terrain is flat. Apart from the pillar and the temple of Mayadevi, there are a number of archaeological remains already exposed which will need conservation before they are incorporated into the design. There are also several modern structures including the old rest house, new tourist hotel, post office, school, etc., which should be removed. Before any landscaping begins, the whole area demands archaeological excavation. The size of the new garden may be increased if desired. The essence of the design must be to create an atmosphere of tranquillity, universality, and extreme clarity consistent with the idea of the birth of Buddhism. Whatever landscaping or planting are done, or whatever structures are made, they must serve this end, and therefore, must be of the highest quality of design, reflecting as it were the whole spirit of man, rather than any sectarian or national bias. (Allchin and Matsushita, 1969, p. 12)

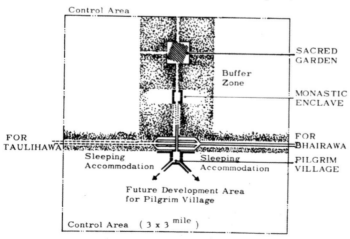

Master plan from Allchin-Matsushita report, 1969

UN brochure 'The birthplace of Buddha' (1970)

In 1970, the ICDL prepared a brochure entitled 'Lumbini. The birthplace of Buddha' for Secretary-General U Thant's appeal to all nations and especially Buddhist countries to provide support for the Development Plan for Lumbini. The brochure stated that:

> Lumbini presents the architect with a formidable challenge. Almost nothing exists today, for even the sal trees have retreated. Everything has to be created there and created in such a way as to reveal the universality of Buddha's message and its significance in the modem world as well as to express the early life of Buddha and the events leading up to the Great Renunciation. The proposals presented here are initial sketches directed towards the achievement of these objectives. They will have to be worked out in considerably more detail within the Master Plan. (United Nations, 1970)

The proposal included five main elements of the future development of Lumbini: the access road from Lumbini to Bhairahawa; the Pilgrim Village; the Green Areas; the Monastic Enclave, and the Sacred Garden. 'The whole design should be animated by a strong and clear-cut concept devoid of any narrow sectarian bias. It should, in fact, express the spirit of the host country of Nepal, whose population embraces both the Hindu and Buddhist faiths, living together in harmony.' (United Nations, 1970)

Pilgrim Village: The Pilgrim Village is to provide accommodation for both pilgrims and tourists on the one hand, and the staff who administer and oversee the Lumbini complex. Conceptually it was essential that the village was not just another tourist centre but an integral part of the entire Lumbini complex and therefore, built to the highest standards of construction. One possible form would have been to have a central open square lying on the main access road from Bhairahawa, surrounded by public services and commercial buildings.

Monastic Enclave: Walking south from the Pilgrim Village in the direction of the Sacred Garden, the visitor would first encounter the Monastic Enclave. It is proposed that this enclave should include a site museum containing the antiquities recovered during the excavations together with other material depicting the life of Buddha. It should also have a small library and information centre, and a group of shrines, monasteries and places of worship to be constructed by individual states and institutions. The area might assume a diversity of styles in keeping with the free development and diversity of Buddhist sects yet preserve an air of tranquillity which would prepare the visitor for the experience of the garden itself.

Green Area: Surrounding the whole site would be 'green areas' whose function would be to surround both the Sacred Garden and Monastic Enclave and separate them from the outside world. Land use in these areas would be strictly controlled and comprise open fields interspersed with groves of trees to provide shelter and wind protection.

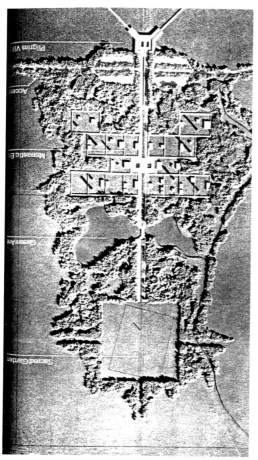

Master plan from UN brochure, 1970

Sacred Garden: It was not possible at that stage to be specific about the treatment of the garden, for much more study and thought would have had to be devoted to this area. The essence of the design should be to create an atmosphere of tranquillity, universality and clarity consistent with the idea of the birth of Buddha. All planting and landscaping would reflect this aim and all structures would have to be built to highest standards of design. Before proceeding further with any detailed plans, it would be essential to make a careful inventory of everything which was presently on the site and conduct a thorough archaeology survey.

UN Lumbini Development Project Report of the Advisory Panel (1971)

In August 1971, the first concept of the design for the Master Plan for Lumbini was presented by Kenzo Tange and his study team to the ICDL Advisory Panel meeting in Tokyo, Japan. According to the agreement between the United Nations and the office of Kenzo Tange and URTEC, the preliminary design of the Master Plan was to be prepared in two stages. In the first stage, the Advisory Panel was to provide comments and recommendations on the study team's general presentation based upon which the concepts were to be prepared for the design. In the second stage, the panel was to review the preliminary designs for Lumbini.

The participants of the panel were representatives of India, Japan, Malaysia, Nepal, Sri Lanka, Thailand, the United Nations and UNDP. The study team from URTEC comprised Kenzo Tange, Sadao Watanabe, Kazuyuki Matsushita, Atsushi Arata and Nachio Trisu.

The report identified the land use controls for the surrounding areas and defined the outline of the area under development. The Lumbini Sacred Garden constituted an area of one by one mile with two additional one by one mile areas due north to be sites for the Monastic Zone and the New Lumbini Village respectively. This area of three square miles was in process to be acquired for the purpose of the Lumbini Development Project by the Government of Nepal. On both sides of the one by three miles strip were areas of one by three miles each and these were declared restricted areas with the option for future integration into the project, thereby assuring for the Lumbini Project a total area of nine square miles. It was suggested that the Government of Nepal should adopt zoning regulations for a total area of twenty five square miles thereby assuring the preservation of existing predominantly agricultural land.

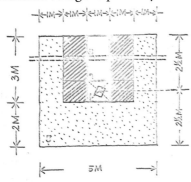

1. – Sacred Garden
2. – Monastic Zone
3. – New Lumbini Village
4. – Restricted Areas
5. – Agricultural Zoned Area (Buffer Zone)

Concept sketch of 5x5 mile Master Plan, 1971

Final outline design for Lumbini (1972)

In 1972, at the meeting of the Advisory Panel, overall layout was adopted. To the northeast, the New Lumbini Village was earmarked for accommodation and service facilities. A central link canal is to connect the New Lumbini Village and the Sacred Garden. This central axis of about two kilometres in length is interspersed with squares as entrances to the cultural centre and the monastic areas. The cultural centre is designed with a library and an archaeological museum. The monasteries would include monks and holy people from international Buddhist communities. The most important problem to be solved in designing the axis was to create a comfortable environment; quiet, protected from the sun; not monotonous, which enables the visitors to walk a long distance without being tired both physically and mentally. Therefore, a narrow canal is proposed in the centre of the axis with pedestrian paths and rows of trees on either side. The running water and the shade of the trees are to make a refreshing environment along the axis. The canal is to enable the use of boats for transportation, though motorized boats are not to be allowed.

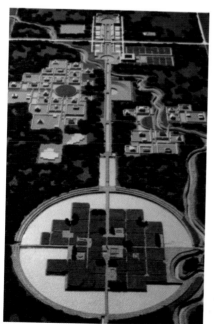

Perspective of the Master Plan in 1972

The excavation and the preservation of ruins is at the centre of the design of the Sacred Garden area because it is in this area that most of the archaeological finds are expected. The design elements of this area are purposely kept flexible. The Sacred Garden is planned with a 1,000 metre circle with the Ashoka Pillar in the centre. A 100 metre square grid system is placed over the area within the circle, which is to be used to align pedestrian paths. The area within the grid is to be either excavated ruins or covered with grass. The Sacred Garden is to be separated from the outside world by being surrounded by water features and forests.

At the first meeting of the Advisory Panel it was decided that no physical symbol should be adopted in the design of the Sacred Garden. The symbolic value of the site was to be reflection of the creation of the garden itself. The basic principle of the design for the garden was to create a quiet natural environment by prohibiting the construction of new structures, with the exception of the Ashoka Pillar and the archaeological findings. However at the second meeting of the Advisory Panel, members felt that a symbol and an area designed for worship might be needed. They decided that as a symbol, the Ashoka Pillar and the remains of the Mayadevi Temple (underneath the present Mayadevi Temple) should be incorporated in a harmonious and unified way. The panel recommended that archaeological research and excavation work should be carried out as the first step of the project so that the essential findings of the excavation could be incorporated into the overall design.

© Durham University/Mark Houshold

Aerial view of the Master Plan along central axis taken in 2012

Master Design for the development of Lumbini (1976-1981)

Phase II, Stage I Report (1976) and Phase II, Stage II Report (1977)

Some major changes to the design were introduced in 1976, which changed the basic concept of the initial plan. The approach to the surrounding area, as well as the existing villages, was very different. There was no rectangular peripheral road and several existing villages were incorporated into the plan. The symmetry of the other plans was lost. The location of the Lumbini Centre was not exactly on the Central Link. The forest only surrounded the buildings and the Sacred Garden and not the entire project site. Instead most of the agricultural land was preserved. Additionally the grid size changed from 100 metres to 80 metres, allowing for more flexible plot sizes, especially in the Monastic Enclave.

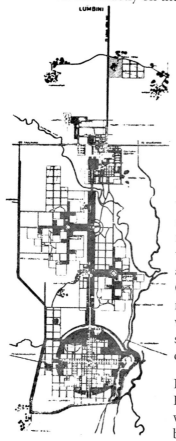

Master plan layout, 1976

The members of the Advisory Panel criticised that the simplicity and clarity of the first concept plan were lost. The Government of Nepal did not want the villages incorporated into the project site. Concerning the Sacred Garden, the response was that the natural and artificial water bodies needed to be kept separate and that the 'road surrounding the Sacred Garden should be placed outside the water network instead of inside. In this way the water network can act as a further barrier separating the Sacred Garden from the outside world'. (Tange and Urtec, 1977, p. 3)

In the design for the Development of Lumbini reflected in the Stage II Report that was submitted in 1977, the design reverted back to the original rectangular shape.

Phase II, Final Report (1978)

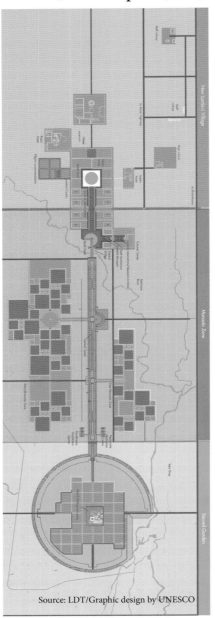

Source: LDT/Graphic design by UNESCO

Final Kenzo Tange Master Plan Layout

As described in the Allchin-Matsushita report of 1969, the most important concept of the Sacred Garden was to create an atmosphere of tranquillity, universality and clarity consistent with the idea of the birth of Buddha. This concept has been basically followed through all alteration of master plans.

In 1978, the final report of Phase II was submitted. This was basically the final shape of the master plan and later only minor changes and adjustments were made. The final plan reverted back to the rigid boarder of the project site as shown in the 1972 plan. The entire master plan area was overlaid with a square grid system of 80 metres. In the monastic zone, a sub-system of 40 metre grids was introduced. The circle around the Sacred Garden was drawn at 800 metres.

Kenzo Tange made every effort to emphasize the values of Lumbini through the master plan. This is evident from the components of the master plan, which have been carefully laid out in direct relation to Buddhism. According to Kenzo Tange, the overall intent is to reinforce the symbolic entity of the Lumbini Garden in its simplicity and clarity. Moreover, the geometric interpretation of the master plan is based on religious symbolism. Interpreting the philosophy of Buddhism and the requirements of the site. The entire five by five miles area is a *mandala*, with the Sacred Garden being the focal point at the centre. The Master Plan mainly consists of circles, squares and lines which are laid out with definite order, proportions and relationships to each other.

The Lumbini Village functions as an entrance area to the ultimate destination, the Sacred Garden, the birthplace of Lord Buddha. It consists of administrative services, which represent worldly life. Therefore, this first component symbolizes the worldly life or impure state of mind of the visitors. The second component is composed of the Cultural Centre and the Monastic Zone, which symbolize understanding of knowledge. The visitors seek knowledge through the library and research centres available in the Cultural Centre. Further south, the Monastic Zone gives an insight into the life of the religious people. Therefore, the visitor gets physically and psychologically prepared to imbibe the religious values of the site. Before progressing towards the holiest place, the Sacred Garden, visitors pass in the vicinity of the meditation centres on either side of the entrance to the Sacred Garden. These meditation centres symbolize the spirituality or purification of the mind before entering the final destination. The Sacred Garden symbolizes enlightenment, while the path from north to south symbolizes the path to nirvana or the attainment of final truth. Besides practical reasons such as environmental cooling and pleasing aesthetics, the circular water body around the Sacred Garden symbolizes the fluid inside the mother's womb. The river, which passes through the Master Plan area, symbolizes the umbilical cord, which connects a baby to its mother.

© Kai Weise

The museum building designed by Kenzo Tange

Conceptual elements of the Kenzo Tange Master Plan

Regional integration

The Kenzo Tange Master Plan has recommended integrating the master plan into the wider economic context and the regional development plan of the Gandaki-Lumbini area. The development of Lumbini was to impact the region through tourism as well as providing service facilities such as a high school, medical centre and cultural facilities. These facilities have been planned with good access from the regional artery, the Taulihawa–Bhairahawa Highway.

Delineation of the site: The project site of one by three mile was decided on by the Government of Nepal even before the Allchin-Matsushita Report. After various proposed alterations, the ridged rectangular shape was finalized. Additionally however, a one by three mile restricted area was added on either side along with an agricultural area covering the remaining parts of a five by five mile area.

Land use plan: Though the shape of the Master Plan changed in each planning phase, the basic structure and layout including the Lumbini Village, Monastic Enclave and Sacred Garden, along with the Central Link, were kept. Within the one by three mile area, the density of land use activities is higher along the central axis. Lumbini Village was earmarked for pilgrim and visitor accommodation. The Monastic Enclave was the site for Buddhist temples of all sects and dominions. This was also the location for monks and nuns to carry out their religious practices. The main archaeological site of the Sacred Garden was encircled by the levee and large water bodies.

Archaeological sites

The protection of potential archaeological sites was the most essential concern of the planners from the beginning. The location of the most important archaeological sites in the Sacred Garden was not clear at that time and so already in the 1972 report, a square grid system of paths was introduced. Only the size of the grid was changed from 100 to 80 metres.

Landscape: The landscape design is contained within the designated forest area which is planned along the edge of the one by three mile project area. This is enhanced by rows of tall Sal trees along the central axis. This is enhanced by water bodies such as the central canal and those around the Sacred Garden. The Sacred Garden has been earmarked to be a predominantly grassed area.

Layout of the major monuments and axis: One of the distinctive characteristics of the Kenzo Tange Master Plan is the strong linear axis dominating the entire area by using topographical and visual features. By utilizing the feature of the Ashoka Pillar and the view of the Himalayan mountain range, the north-south axis provides the spine of the site.

Transportation system: The main entrance to the site was designed at the crossing point of the central axis and the Taulihawa-Bhairahawa Highway.

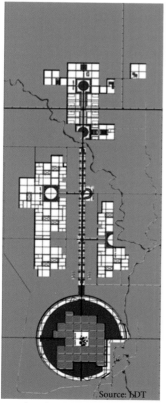

Plan of built and natural environment

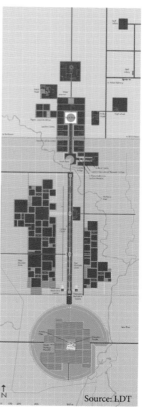

Zoning plansof Lumbini

Visitors were supposed to move along the central axis passing through the Monastic Zone to the Sacred Garden either on foot or by using boats provided on the central canal. The vehicular service roads were provided from a gate along the periphery of the one by three mile area, keeping vehicular and pedestrian traffic entirely separated. The aim was to provide a quiet environment.

Approach to Sacred Garden: Kenzo Tange's idea was to create an 'enlightening experience' when moving from the north entrance to the Sacred Garden. The Lumbini Village area with the Lumbini centre was planned on the main highway which included accommodation and commercial facilities. This was the point, where visitors were to leave their daily life behind and enter a more spiritual world. The atmosphere for visitors was to change from the mundane to the sacred. The design also allowed for a gradient from an artificial built up area to a natural landscape. From an area predominantly of brick buildings, the central canal introduces rows of trees. This then leads to the Sacred Garden which was to be surrounded by water, with paths of top soil and a landscape covered with grass. The visitors were to be guided by the Ashoka Pillar to the Sacred Garden and by the Himalayan mountain range when departing.

Monastic Zone: The Monastic Zone consists of two monastic enclaves; one in the west for Mahayana and the other in the east for Hinayana schools of Buddhism. There are 42 plots with the provision of future extensions of up to 104 plots. There are three types of square plots: A of 160 metres; B of 120 metres; and C of 80 metres. The design control system in the Monastic Zone uses a common framework of squares, pedestrian walkways, fences, walls, entrance courts and service yards, within which individual architecture can be realized with both flexibility and unity within the whole area. The buildings were not to be built higher than three storeys.

The Sacred Garden: No structure other than the archaeological site should be allowed in the Sacred Garden. All modern structures existing in this area were to be removed and only historically authenticated archaeological vestiges were to be conserved. A grid system comprising of 80 × 80 metres was to mark the pathways and plots for archaeological survey. The layout was to be considered flexible to adjust to changing requirements without altering the basic concept. However, the use of bricks would be forbidden in the Sacred Garden.

Sacred Garden as per the Master Plan

It was a key issue for the Master Plan on how to deal with the potential archaeological areas which had not yet been excavated. This factor of uncertainty was solved by Kenzo Tange using a grid system. This he describes in a book published in 1980.

Archaeologists place great hope for finds in the vicinity of the garden, though thorough excavations have yet to be carried out. Many people felt that it was necessary to erect something in the centre of the garden that would serve as a symbol. But we did not agree. Our proposal is to surround and protect the area from which archaeological finds are expected to be forthcoming by means of a pond laid out to suggest the mandala (a Buddhist graphic representation of the cosmos). Within this area, a grid of walkways is to be planned at intervals of 80 metres. Visitors are permitted to walk only on these paths. The ground is left undisturbed until archaeologists have a chance to dig. The things uncovered in their excavation will themselves serve as monuments. Nothing new will be added to the site at all. We have received approval for this proposal, which is an example of the importance of protecting things and places of historical importance. (Tange, 1980)

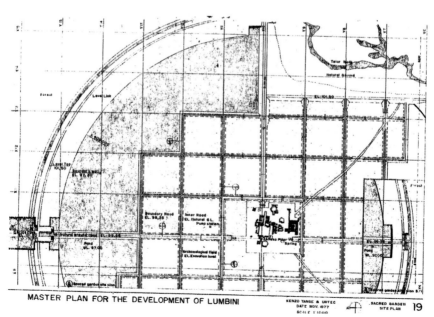

MASTER PLAN FOR THE DEVELOPMENT OF LUMBINI

Detailed plan of the Sacred Garden

According to Kenzo Tange, the basic principle of design for the Sacred Garden is to create a quiet, natural environment by prohibiting the construction of new structures and by eliminating and relocating the existing structures, with the exception of the Ashoka Pillar. The Sacred Garden should be composed of the Sacred Area, the Tank Area and the Forest Area. The Master Plan proposed to provide a very minimum of service facilities in the Sacred Garden Area for the pilgrims and tourists. The archaeological office and the utility block were to be constructed at the eastern portion of the levee embankment.

The Sacred Garden is the focal point of the Lumbini Garden to symbolize the birth space of the Lord Buddha. The form of a circle enclosing squares embodies the mystic symbol of the universe in the Buddhism with purity and simplicity. The sacred area surrounded by the pond and a circular levee link to protect against the inundation is not permitted to accommodate any kind of construction to preserve its archaeological value, and introduced only with the design elements of the pedestrian grid and its approach system to an excavation unit. These elements should have appropriate dimensions and positions to retain the conservation of excavated or unexcavated areas undamaged. (Tange and Urtec, 1978, pp. 19-20)

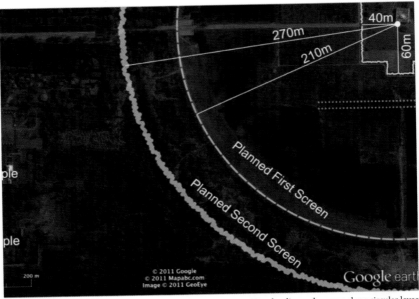

Visual radius and screens along circular levee

In the design of the garden, two elements are incorporated: the unearthed ancient urban structure; and a system grid for archaeological surveys. The system for archaeological surveys consists of parallel roads running on an 80 metres grid in either north-south or east-west directions. Each unit of an 80 by 80 metres lot is defined by the roads and forms a basic field unit for archaeological surveying. These roads will be utilized as service roads. The surface of the road is covered by topsoil with loose gravel. Potential areas for archaeological discovery are widely dispersed in the whole area and the construction of roads or levees should take this into account. When an unexpected discovery occurs in critical areas, the layout can be modified without altering the basic system. The modification may include the use of bridges over significant archaeological remains. The use of bricks is strictly forbidden in the Sacred Areas.

The physical design of the Sacred Area is also conditioned by the technical need for water management. The dominant natural features of the site are the rivers – the Hathaway, Ghurkha and Telar – which flow through it. They are mostly dry between October and May. During the rainy season, they flood the surrounding regions. As an integral component of the archaeological preservation plan, a circular levee link is to be built around the excavation area to protect it from flooding. In order to conserve the natural aspect of Telar *Nadi*, which is itself a historical monument, a south east segment of the levee link would be modified to keep its natural shape.

An excavated pond area lies inside the levee link with a low water level to facilitate drainage from the excavation area. The level of the levee link is set at 101.5 metres and the water level is at 97.00 metres (three metres below the base level of the Ashoka Pillar). The water in the Sacred Pond is fed by the link pond through a pipe. The water level of the link pond is 99 metres. The four quadrants of the tank are also inter-connected. The gate structure at the southern corner maintains the water level at 97 metres during the dry and rainy seasons. On the top of the levee link is a four metres wide circuit road with edges lined with curb stones. Both sides of the circuit road are graded and they are surfaced with grass to provide a continuous foliage cover over the levee and to protect it from water erosion.

Architectural Design for the Lumbini Garden

1979 Phase III, Stage I

The initial architectural designs and detailing of various components of the project area were prepared.

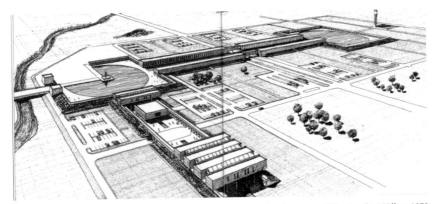

Perspective of cultural centre and New Lumbini Village 1979

Perspective of central axis in New Lumbini Village 1979

1981 Phase III, Stage II

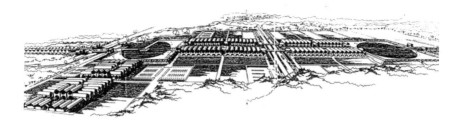

Perspective of cultural centre and New Lumbini Village 1981

Perspective of central axis in New Lumbini Village 1981

1981 Master Design for the Lumbini Garden (draft)

The draft document provided details on the design of the Lumbini Centre, Cultural Centre, Central Link and Sacred Garden. In order to create inter-relationships among the various functions and activities and to organize the various movements and activities of visitors, an integrated arcade space was introduced into the plan. In the Lumbini Centre, an arcade was thought desirable along both sides of the Central Canal with the necessary facilities placed behind these arcades. Trees were not to be planted around the buildings of the Lumbini Centre and the Cultural Centre. This had the purpose of providing an unobstructed view of these buildings from a distance and to strengthen their impression as a gate to the Lumbini Garden for visitors who arrive via the Bhairahawa-Lumbini Road. The layout of the southwest corner of the Sacred Garden around the village mound was also revised.

Major changes during planning phase (1969 to 1981)

The plan was developed over the period starting with discussions even before the Allchin-Matsushita Report of 1969. The land use control around the main one by three mile project area was already proposed in these initial stages. In the report of the Advisory panel in 1971, Kenzo Tange proposed a five by five mile agricultural zoned area including a three by three mile restricted area. The land use control was officially stated in the 1971 Final Outline Design for Lumbini. In a later report in 1978 and 1981, the land use control for the surrounding areas seemed to have been ignored.

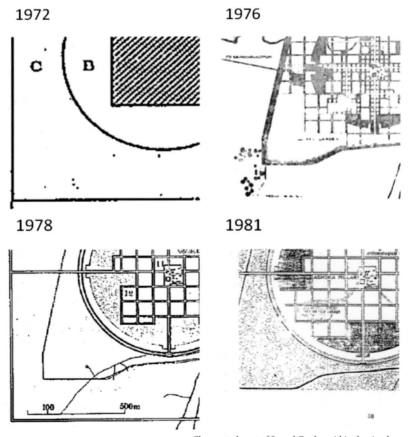

1972   1976

1978   1981

Changes to layout of Sacred Garden within the circular pond

Some of the main aspects of the design that changed during the planning phase were the boundary of the project site and the response to the surrounding areas. Initially the design incorporated a hundred metre grid for the Sacred Garden which was then extended over the entire planning area. This was later changed to an eighty metre grid. Accordingly, the size of the circular levee around the Sacred Garden changed from a thousand metres to eight hundred metres. Along with this change, the shape of the Sacred Garden and the water body were repeatedly modified as knowledge of the archaeological site improved.

The Sacred Garden was to be developed to provide access and information to visitors on the archaeological remains within the area. Through archaeological investigations, the total picture of built structures and their transitions would need to be known. The question was raised regarding what level of artefacts were to be shown to the public, as several layers of remains existed in each area.

However concerning the Village Mound in the south west, it was assumed that little would have remained from the village structures since the building materials had very little time-resistant qualities. It was considered desirable that after archaeological investigations were completed, some sort of landscaping be carried out to show above the ground the unique village pattern of this area to develop it as a public space. Also, the ancient road pattern should be reconstructed. The position of the levee and the water body was tentative. The exact extent of this area and the surrounding water body was only going to be determined through archaeological investigations.

© Kai Weise

Peace Stupa

Major changes during implementation phase and critical review of Master Plan

Over the years, there have been various changes that have been adopted and implemented. There has been some construction work, which has not followed the basic essence of the Master Plan. For example, the Peace Stupa located within the Lumbini Centre and the boundary wall were not part of the original design. Within the Monastic Zone, some of the monasteries have been constructed against set regulations on height and axial relations.

The existing approach to planning for the area within the levee is not clear. There is a general agreement that the Master Plan needs to be followed, however this has a major impact on the World Heritage Property. The road network based on an 80 by 80 metre grid does not seem appropriate for conserving a World Heritage Property. Additionally, the potential archaeological areas are not clearly demarcated to secure them from possible threats. The question of demolishing existing structures within the Sacred Garden is still under discussion, especially in respect to the two existing monasteries within the Sacred Garden.

Further discussions are required in respect to the planning of the Sacred Garden area beyond the levee. This area can be developed into a forest and could accommodate various functional requirements that need to be removed from the Inner Sacred Garden, the World Heritage area and the Buffer Zone.

Due to the fact that the implementation of the Kenzo Tange Master Plan has been slow, it has provided the opportunity for serious scrutiny concerning both functional attributes as well as the philosophical concept. The practical aspects have restricted themselves to the required infrastructure and services for visitor numbers that are much higher than originally calculated. There have also been discussions on the forms of transportation for the visitors along the central canal. Beyond these more functional aspects of the Master Plan, criticism has arisen concerning the Kenzo Tange decision to make the Ashoka Pillar the focal point and provide a central axis towards the north. According to Sudarshan Raj Tiwari, the focal point and geometric centre of the plan should have been the exact birth spot as indicated by the Nativity Sculpture. This was further supported by the discovery of the Marker Stone during the excavations in 1994. Furthermore, the north-south axis was introduced, ignoring the importance given to the east-west axis in previous phases of developments around the birth spot of Lord Buddha.

© Kai Weise

The central axis with the Ashoka Pillar, the Peace Stupa and a newly erected baby Buddha statue, 2013

© Bernard Grismayer

Perception Five

One of the most significant places of one of the world's greatest religions. Lumbini as a World Heritage Property

Lumbini's central area of 130 by 150 metres was inscribed on the List of World Heritage in 1997 with the remaining part of the inner Sacred Garden designated as the buffer zone. The possible modification of the boundaries has been discussed since 2005 to include the entire Inner Sacred Garden within the boundaries of the World Heritage Property and to extend the buffer zone to the entire outer Sacred Garden. The conservation approach for Lumbini must be based on the overall objective of preserving the Outstanding Universal Value of the property.

Content

History of the World Heritage nomination; Perceptions and reactions to nomination. Attributes and elements of Outstanding Universal Value. Statement of Outstanding Universal Value. Boundary, buffer zone and zones of influence. Management challenges. Lumbini's World Heritage status and the Kenzo Tange Master Plan. Relation to territorial heritage.

References

This chapter is based on contributions by Herb Stovel. Reference is also attributed to contributions by Basanta Bidari and Kai Weise.

History of the World Heritage nomination

The initial nomination of 'Lumbini and associated sites' was submitted to the World Heritage Committee in 1993. This original nomination was deferred by the World Heritage Bureau at its seventeenth Session in June 1993.

> The Bureau recommended that the inscription of this property on the World Heritage List be deferred until the Nepalese authorities provide precise information on conservation measures and site management which are in conformity with international standards. Also, as a prerequisite for the future examination of the nomination, the Bureau requested the competent authorities to supply an Indicative List of properties that Nepal might wish to propose for inscription in the future (World Heritage Committee, 1993, p. 38).

> The original nomination of 1993 included a number of separate archaeological sites associated with the life and work of the Lord Buddha. Two of these, Kapilavastu (Tilaurakot), where the Lord Buddha lived as Prince Siddhartha before his enlightenment, and Ramagrama, the only relic stupa not opened by Asoka, … ICOMOS … is of the opinion that the current state of knowledge, conservation, and management of both is not sufficiently advanced to permit them being included in the present nomination. It recommends, therefore, that this should await the completion of the program of non-destructive archaeological investigation, using geophysical techniques … and the preparation of satisfactory conservation and management plans. Once this work has been completed, the State Party should be invited to submit the two sites as extensions to an existing inscribed site of Lumbini, with a change of title indicating the association of all three with the life and work of the Lord Buddha (ICOMOS, 1993, p. 80).

A new nomination under the title 'Lumbini, the Birthplace of the Lord Buddha' was submitted to the World Heritage Committee in June 1996. The new nomination was reviewed by ICOMOS in September 1996 and the recommendation was made to inscribe the property on the basis of criteria (iii) and (vi). Criterion (iii) requires the heritage property to 'bear a unique or at least exceptional testimony to a cultural tradition or to a civilization which is living or which has disappeared.' Criterion (iv) requires the heritage property to 'be directly or tangibly associated with events or living traditions, with ideas, or with beliefs, with artistic and literary works of outstanding universal significance' (World Heritage Committee, 2011, pp. 20-21).

The World Heritage Committee inscribed Lumbini on the List of World Heritage on 6 December 1997 during its 21st session with following annotations:

> The Committee decided to inscribe this site on the basis of criteria (iii) and (vi). As the birthplace of the Lord Buddha, the sacred area of Lumbini is one of the holiest places of one of the world's great religions, and its remains contain important evidence about the nature of Buddhist pilgrimage centres from a very early period. The Delegate of Thailand declared that apart from Lumbini, there are two other sites closely associated with Buddha, which are in the process of preparation to be presented as serial nominations and that he hoped that the Committee would consider them in this context (World Heritage Committee, 1997, p. 46).

Remains of nomastries in the Sacred Garden

Perceptions and reactions to the nomination

The inscription of Lumbini on the World Heritage list was considered by many as an international certification that Lord Buddha was born in Nepal, which would make earlier discussions on the national ownership of the site obsolete. However, considering that today's state borders did not exist at the time of Lord Buddha's birth, these debates appear to be rather rhetorical. Since the 're-discovery' of Lumbini and of the essential inscription on the Ashoka Pillar, the position of Lumbini and thereby the birthplace of Lord Buddha has not been seriously questioned.

The inclusion of the sites of Tilaurakot and Ramagrama in the initial nomination dossier of 1993 further underlined the intent of international recognition of these important sites linked to the life of the historical Buddha. These two sites were placed on the tentative list for World Heritage but not included in the nomination dossier submitted in 1996. However, when Lumbini was inscribed on the World Heritage list during the 21st session of the World Heritage Committee in 1997, some participants, notably the Delegate of Thailand, underlined the importance of the link between Lumbini, Tilaurkaot and Ramagrama.

The inscription of Lumbini on the World Heritage list also underlined the importance of conservation within an area determined for development of an international religious centre and site of pilgrimage. Through the nomination, the Government of Nepal, as State Party to the World Heritage Convention, made a clear commitment to safeguard the attributes that express Outstanding Universal Value. At the same time, many stakeholders were conscious of the fact that international and local interest in contributing to the beautification and ornamentation of the archaeological site would entail the risk of an inappropriate competition between donors, each trying to construct larger and more intrusive structures in and around the sacred site.

The relative control of such activities continues to demonstrate the effectiveness of the World Heritage inscription. This has however also led to complaints by some local officials and potential donors that UNESCO is not allowing any kind of improvement to the site, thereby ignoring the obligation of the State Party to respect the provisions of the World Heritage Convention

Attributes and elements of Outstanding Universal Value

There are various elements that are specifically mentioned in the Nomination Document as being of Outstanding Universal Value. The complex of structures within the archaeological conservation area that is the subject of this nomination consists of the following:

- The S[.]akya Tank, in which Mayadevi bathed before giving birth to the Lord Buddha, within the Mayadevi Temple enclosure. The original temple was built before the visit of Ashoka in 249 [BCE] and probably consisted of no more than a platform constructed on the cross-wall system, later converted into a *shikara* temple. The 20th century temple has now been demolished, leaving on display the remains of brick structures dating from the 3rd century [BCE] to the present century.

- The sandstone As[.]oka Pillar with its Sanskrit inscriptions, that of As[.] okan *brahmi* script and the later one of Ripu Malla in *devanagari* script.

- The excavated remains of Buddhist *viharas* (monasteries) of the 3rd century [BCE] to the 5th century [CE]. The rectangular pool between them dates back to the 20th century.

- The remains of Buddhist stupas (memorial shrines) from the 3rd century [BCE] to the 15th century [CE] (ICOMOS, 1996, p. 79)

© Kai Weise

Since the inscription of Lumbini onto the World Heritage List there have been various archaeological excavations and surveys that have revealed numerous new findings or clarified earlier theories. One of the important new finds was the Marker Stone which was not yet discovered at the time of inscription. In addition to these elements, there are clearly further archaeological sites that are linked to this central area. The potential archaeological sites extend at least toward the north and southeast of the inscribed site. The village mound that has been identified towards the southwest is clearly an early village that existed during the lifetime of Siddhartha Gautama. The extent of archaeological remains spread out even beyond the buffer zone defined by the surrounding water body, since an early well has been found towards the southwest beyond the village mound. It is today known as the 'nursery well', since it is located in the garden nursery of the Lumbini Development Trust.

> The Sacred Area that forms the nominated property lies within a modern circular feature defined by a moat and this in turn forms part of a modern monumental pilgrimage centre based on two monasteries. Outside the nominated area, but within the buffer zone, there are other religious buildings of the 20th century and buildings in use by the Lumbini Development Trust, all of which are scheduled for demolition. (ICOMOS, 1996, p. 79)

In addition to the unique archaeological vestiges, an important attribute is the characteristics of the site as pilgrimage site probably since the lifetime of Gautama Siddhartha. This also contributes to Lumbini being of Outstanding Universal Value. It is therefore essential that Lumbini continues being a site of pilgrimage.

© Kai Weise

Statement of Outstanding Universal Value

Since 2007, all World Heritage Properties are required to prepare statements of Outstanding Universal Value (OUV), which allow for a clear understanding of the property at the time of inscription. The statement must define why the property is considered to be of OUV, thereby giving direction to management by defining the attributes that need to be retained in order to sustain OUV. The retrospective Statement of OUV for Lumbini was prepared during the establishment to the integrated management system and submitted to the World Heritage Committee during the second cycle of periodic reporting on the implementation of the World Heritage Convention in 2011. The World Heritage Committee at its thirtysixth session at Saint Petersbourg in 2012 adopted the retrospective Statement of OUV of 'Lumbini, the birthplace of Lord Buddha' (World Heritage Committee , 2012).

Lumbini, the birthplace of Lord Buddha (NEPAL)

666   1997   C (iii) (vi)

Brief Synthesis:

Lord Buddha was born in 623 BCE in the sacred area of Lumbini located in the Terai plains of southern Nepal, testified by the inscription on the pillar erected by the Mauryan Emperor Ashoka in 249 BCE. Lumbini is one of the holiest places of one of the world's great religions and its remains contain important evidence about the nature of Buddhist pilgrimage centres from as early as the 3rd century BCE.

The complex of structures within the archaeological conservation area includes the Sakya Pond (*Pushkarani*), the remains within the Mayadevi Temple consisting brick structures in a cross-wall system dating from the 3rd century BCE to the present century and the sandstone Ashoka Pillar with its *Pali* inscriptions in *Brahmi* script. Additionally, there are the excavated remains of Buddhist *viharas* (monasteries) of the 3rd century BCE to the 5th century CE and the remains of Buddhist stupas (memorial shrines) from the 3rd century BCE to the 15th century CE The site is now being developed as a Buddhist pilgrimage centre in which the archaeological remains associated with the birth of Lord Buddha form a central feature.

Criterion (iii):

As the birthplace of Lord Buddha, testified by the inscription on the Ashoka Pillar, the sacred area in Lumbini is one of the most holy and significant places for one of the world's great religions.

Criterion (vi):

The archaeological remains of Buddhist *viharas* (monasteries) and stupas (memorial shrines) from the 3rd century BCE to the 15th century CE provide important evidence about the nature of Buddhist pilgrimage centres from a very early period.

Integrity:

The integrity of Lumbini has been achieved by means of preserving the archaeological remains that give the property its OUV within the boundaries. The significant attributes and elements of the property have been preserved. The Buffer Zone gives the property a further layer of protection. Further excavations of potential archaeological sites and appropriate protection of the archaeological remains are of high priority for the integrity of the site. The boundaries, however, do not include the entire archaeological area and various sites found in the Buffer Zone. The entire property is owned by the Government of Nepal and is being managed by the Lumbini Development Trust (LDT) and therefore there is little threat of development or neglect. However, the effects of industrial development in the region have been identified as a risk to the integrity of the property.

Authenticity:

The authenticity of the archaeological remains within the boundaries has been confirmed through a series of excavations since the discovery of the Ashoka Pillar in 1896. The remains of *viharas*, stupas and numerous layers of brick structures from the 3rd century BCE to the present century at the site of the Mayadevi Temple are proof of Lumbini already having been a centre of pilgrimage from early times. The archaeological remains require active conservation and monitoring to ensure that the impact of natural degradation, influence of humidity and the effect of the visitors are kept under control. The property continues to express its OUV through its archaeological remains. The delicate balance must be maintained between conserving the archaeological vestiges of the property while providing for the pilgrims.

Management

The property is protected as per the Ancient Monument Preservation Act 1956. The site management is carried out by the Lumbini Development Trust (LDT), an autonomous and non-profit making organization. The entire site is owned by the Government of Nepal. The property falls within the centre of the Master Plan area, the planning of which was initiated together with the United Nations and carried out by Kenzo Tange between 1972 and 1978.

The long-term challenges for the protection and management of the property are to control the impact of the visitors and natural impacts such as humidity and industrial development in the region. A management plan is in the process of being developed to ensure the long-term safeguarding of the archaeological vestiges of the property, while allowing for the property to continue being visited by pilgrims and tourists from around the world (Lumbini Development Trust, 2011).

© Kai Weise

Ancient brickwork and visitors inside the Mayadevi Temple taken in 2008

Boundary, buffer zone and zones of influence

The World Heritage boundary encompasses an area of 130 by 150 metres which includes the Ashoka Pillar, the Shakya Pond and the archaeological vestiges of *viharas* and stupas around the Mayadevi Shelter. It however does not include extensions of these archaeological sites to the north and the southeast. Furthermore, the boundary does not encompass the Village Mound towards the southwest area.

The World Heritage Buffer Zone is defined by the area within the water body as demarcated in the Kenzo Tange Master Plan. At the time of inscription the water body had not yet been excavated. It was assumed that such a radical intrusion within the existing natural surrounds would hardly have been allowed within the Buffer Zone and therefore this area was excluded. However, for the long-term protection of the World Heritage Property, the entire Sacred Garden area would need to be maintained as a forested area as a shield from the pressures of surrounding developments.

The Ancient Monument Preservation Act 1956 is the primary legislation for 'preserving ancient monuments and … controlling the trade in archaeological objects as well as the excavation of the place of ancient monuments and by acquiring and preserving ancient monuments and archaeological, historical or artistic objects'. As a World Heritage Property, Lumbini requires the highest level of national protection. The archaeological vestiges come under the direct protection of this act. Further protection would be provided by the Ancient Monument Preservation Act through the possibility of declaring an area a 'Protected Monument Zone', possibly the entire Sacred Garden of Lumbini, comprising an area of 1600 by 1360 metres. This area would be strictly protected from any inappropriate developments, especially those that might threaten the OUV of the World Heritage Property. The extent of this area is clearly defined. Adjoining to the north is the monastic zone of Kenzo Tange's Master Plan. To the east is the straight road from Parsa to Lankapur. To the south is the straight road from Lankapur to Padariya Chowk. To the west is the straight road from Padariya Chowk to Lokaria Chowk.

Management challenges

A World Heritage Property is by definition a highly valued site, which attracts people having various motives. They are curious tourists, devoted pilgrims or visitors wanting to contribute to or profit from these important places. Even those with the best of intentions, when visiting or contributing to the maintenance, conservation or development, will have a certain impact on the heritage property. When visiting the site tourists and pilgrims might trample over things, touch them, feel them, smell them and possibly make offerings. They might chant, sing, meditate, observe or read. Those, who want to invest in the heritage site would like to improve the infrastructure and services and provide new activities. They might also want to create monumental structures for merit or introduce profitable businesses. Though inevitable and not necessarily unwanted, these activities need to be monitored to ensure that the impact does not impact the heritage in a negative or irreversible manner.

Every World Heritage Property requires a clearly defined management system.

> To be deemed of Outstanding Universal Value, a property must also meet the conditions of integrity and/or authenticity and must have an adequate protection and management system to ensure its safeguarding. (World Heritage Committee, 2011, p. 21)

The management process for Lumbini was developed through consensus of the concerned authorities. Discussions have been held since 2006, with a series of specific workshops carried out between August 2011 and January 2012 as part of the UNESCO/Japanese Funds-in-Trust project 'Strengthening conservation and management of Lumbini, the birthplace of Lord Buddha'.

The Integrated Management Process must be seen as a road map towards achieving the goal of conserving the OUV of Lumbini. The primary objective of the Integrated Management Process of Lumbini is to protect the OUV of the World Heritage Property as well as to ensure that Lumbini becomes the catalyst for the sustainable development of the Historic Buddhist Region.

Four principles were identified that are to be observed in achieving the management goals. 'significance driven' is the concern for the conservation of the significance of the site. This is at the core of the decision-making process and it must be balanced against the interests of other sectors. An 'integrated approach' is the integrated management style that will follow a systemic and holistic approach to conservation, taking into account the significance of the monuments, the cultural and natural context, within which they are found, and the living heritage that lends them their local value. 'Process oriented' is the integrated management style that will focus on the processes and linkages between the components of the site and the various actors to allow realistic long-term implementation. 'Sustainability' indicates that the integrated management approach will be prepared and implemented based on an understanding of sustainability: economic, social, environmental, as well as cultural values.

Key objectives for managing Lumbini

1. To identify the attributes and elements that give Lumbini its OUV, define authenticity and integrity for the site and possibly redefine the boundaries and Buffer Zones.

2. To prepare a plan that provides guidelines and regulations for the physical development of the entire Sacred Garden which ensures the preservation of its OUV; provides for the requirements of pilgrims and visitors; an appropriate environment; and identifies the means of implementing the plan.

3. To determine an appropriate long-term solution for safeguarding the archaeological vestiges in and around the Mayadevi Temple which includes an in-depth understanding of the threats to the archaeological remains and appropriate provisions for pilgrims, and to identify the means of implementing this solution.

4. To carry out detailed archaeological investigations of the highest scientific standard including documentation and analysis, the provision of appropriate and adequate means of conserving the archaeological remains within the Sacred Garden and where necessary throughout the Master Plan area, to identify the means of implementing these projects.

5. To provide for the needs of the pilgrims, taking into account the impact these activities and required facilities have on other visitors, the archaeological remains and the authenticity and integrity of the

Sacred Garden, and to identify the means of implementing these provisions.

6. To determine the means of implementing the Kenzo Tange Master Plan, as the basis for defining the development in the five by five mile area around the World Heritage Property.

7. To redefine the Lumbini World Heritage Site boundaries and Buffer Zone, considering the preparation of the Tentative List sites of Tilaurakot and Ramagrama for nomination and placing further important Buddhist sites on the Tentative List.

8. To carry out archaeological research and conservation throughout the Historic Buddhist Region, stretching from Lumbini to Tilaurakot and Ramagrama and the establishment of an integrated plan and to provide for the implementation of the plan.

9. To identify the means of ensuring the appropriate development of the Historic Buddhist Region by prioritizing conservation.

10. To facilitate strategies for poverty alleviation of the local communities and to develop tourism by means of improving facilities, services, infrastructure and accessibility of heritage sites in the Historic Buddhist Region.

11. To ensure the serenity and sanctity of the Buddhist sites in and around Lumbini by protecting the environment, controlling the threat of natural disasters and introducing legal provisions and means of enforcing them.

12. To establish coordination between all international partners, national authorities and site managers.

13. To review the status of the Lumbini Development Trust, its objectives, authority and obligations to manage a World Heritage Property and initiate the amendment of the LDT Act and bylaws accordingly.

14. To establish a World Heritage Management Office within the Lumbini Development Trust which includes a database to coordinate, compile and make accessible information related to the Lumbini World Heritage Property.

(Government of Nepal, 2012, p. 8)

Lumbini's World Heritage status and the Kenzo Tange Master Plan

The existence of the Kenzo Tange Master Plan was an important element in Lumbini's nomination as a World Heritage Property.

At the time of inscription, the water bodies around the inner Sacred Garden had not yet been excavated. It was therefore considered prudent not to include this area requiring major development to be placed within the World Heritage area and not even within the buffer zone. The buffer zone was therefore outlined along the planned inner boundaries of the water body as defined in the Kenzo Tange Master Plan. This required the World Heritage boundaries to be reduced to an area of 130 by 150 metres, containing only the main archaeological vestiges around the Ashoka Pillar.

This strategy did allow for Lumbini to be inscribed on the World Heritage list without any misgivings from the advisory bodies or the World Heritage Committee. The boundaries however did not include all the historical sites in Lumbini. There are several other archaeologically important areas, most importantly the area known as the Village Mound to the southwest corner of the inner Sacred Garden. Recent research provides evidence for an earlier hypothesis that this area covers the ancient Lumbini village referred to in the Ashoka Pillar inscription. Even further to the southwest, outside the circular levee, an ancient well was found which might have indicated the alignment of an ancient route. This important archaeological element was not considered by the Kenzo Tange Master Plan, but might have needed to be part of the World Heritage Property to ensure integrity.

Safeguarding Lumbini depends on controlling development in and around the Sacred Garden. This can only be achieved by ensuring full implementation of the Kenzo Tange Master Plan. First of all, it is important to strengthen the association between the 'archaeological footprint' and the OUV of the property. Additionally, there needs to be correlation between the sacred values identified by Kenzo Tange and the specific Outstanding Universal Value recognized by the World Heritage Committee with its inscription of the property. This link needs to be researched and clearly proven since properties are not inscribed for the potential OUV, but for their ability to explicitly demonstrate Outstanding Universal Value.

An extended 'zone of influence' encompasses the full five by five mile Kenzo Tange Master Plan, which is related to the mechanisms required to maintain the relationship and quality of the integrity of the setting for the inscribed zone. The concept of 'zone of influence' is increasingly being recognized as legitimate in World Heritage Committee discussions, given the number of high rise structures outside recognized buffer zones, which threaten the integrity of the Outstanding Universal Value of inscribed World Heritage Properties. There is no doubt that out of scale and out of place structures already constructed, and planned for construction in the five by five mile zone adversely impact the OUV of the already inscribed property and its associated buffer zone. There is a close link between safeguarding the World Heritage Property and the implementation of the entire Kenzo Tange Master Plan. The impact of development activities beyond the inscribed zone would be managed through guidelines that consider disturbance of potential archaeological resources, construction height, scale, proximities to other features, controls on defined sight lines and view planes and architectural design. These should not be too prescriptive, but rather reinforce general principles already established in the Kenzo Tange Master Plan and the Operational Guidelines for Implementation of the World Heritage Convention.

The circular pond around the inner Sacred Garden

Relation to territorial heritage

Lumbini is closely linked to the heritage found over a territory spanning across three districts (Kapilvastu, Rupendehi and Nawalparasi) encompassing an area of about 80 by 25 km. At present, the Lumbini inscription is built around the central idea that the site is the birthplace of Lord Buddha. The area around the inscribed zone contains significant archaeological resources, as well as elsewhere within the Sacred Garden. While expert consensus exists around the importance of Ramagrama (as the only unplundered relic *stupa* associated with the Buddha), the site's hinterland could yield much important information about the use and chronology of the site. Tilaurakot is considered to be the site of Buddha's father's family and 'one of best preserved urban forms and environs of any provincial city within the early historic archaeology of South Asia' (Coningham, 2009, p. 15), however much more remains to be learned about the origins and evolution of the site.

The Integrated Management Framework document for Lumbini touches upon the planning of this territory as the historic Buddhist region. 'The governance of the Historic Buddhist Region will be carried out under special provisions adopted by the Government of Nepal. Development will take place based on the concept of conserving the heritage sites, particularly the numerous archaeological sites in the region. An appropriate system of governance will be established to ensure the sustainable development of the regions spanning across the three districts of Kapilvastu, Rupendehi and Nawalparasi' (Government of Nepal, 2012, p. 10).

The understanding of the historic Buddhist region in Nepal and the subsequent recognition of the importance of conservation and development depends on the results of future archaeological survey work and on the thematic orientation chosen. For example, the region could be understood to be based on the diverse key sites in the life of the Lord Buddha and afterwards: Lord Buddha's birthplace (Lumbini) Lord Buddha's father's home where Lord Buddha remained until 29 years of age (Tilaurakot) and the most intact stupa of those eight stupas built to hold his relics (Ramagrama). There is however also the theme of the birthplaces of the three Buddhas, each site commemorated with an Ashoka Pillar: Siddhartha Gautama in Lumbini, Kanakamuni in Gotihawa and Krakuchanda in Niglihawa. A further theme is comprised of the early Chinese Buddhist pilgrim sites commemorating the pilgrimage route associated with Buddha, which were used and developed by visiting Chinese pilgrims. The nature of the OUV for these various combinations of sites, or the individual sites which could be nominated on their own merits, would need to be adequately and accurately defined with further study and analysis carried out, along with defining the boundaries in preparing for possible new nominations.

In addition it is important to note that the historic Buddhist region stretches across the border into Northern India. This is home to other sacred sites, where Gautama Buddha was enlightened (Bodhagaya), where he preached his first sermon (Sarnath), and where he attained *mahāparinirvāna* (Kushinagara). Mahabodhi Temple Complex at Bodhgaya is a World Heritage Property, Sarnath is on the World Heritage Tentative List, while Kusinagara has not yet been identified for World Heritage nomination.

Fortification wall of Tilaurakot

© Bernard Grismayer

Perception Six

A place in a sacred landscape at risk. The environment of Lumbini

The Sacred Garden mirrors the importance of the natural environment in the life of Lord Buddha. Its physical planning must take into account not only historical, religious aspects but also the natural environment. The 'garden' or 'forest' must retain a natural balance, considering the climate, hydrology and fauna and flora of the region to create a sacred landscape.

Content

Gautama Buddha, the forests and the Sarus cranes. Buddhism and nature. Flora. Fauna. Water and soil characteristics. Climatic conditions. Managing the natural resources and the environment. Environmental Impact Assessment of industrial development around Lumbini.

References

This chapter is based on contributions by Rajendra Suwal, Ukesh Bhuju and Anil Chitrakar. Reference has also been taken from contributions by Basanta Bidari and Kai Weise.

Gautama Buddha, the forests and the sarus cranes

Literature mentions that Lumbini was a beautiful, pleasurable or recreational garden (known as Lumbini *Kannan*, Lumbini *Vatika*, Lumbini *Upavana*, Lumbini *Pradimokshavana*, Lumbini *Chittalatavana*, etc.). The garden was collectively maintained by both the Sakyas and the Koliyas during the lifetime of Lord Buddha.

Siddhartha Gautama was born in a forest clearing or garden. He spent six years wandering the forests before he became enlightened under a Bodhi Tree in Bodhgaya. He then spent the rest of his life, some 45 years, wandering in the forests. He gave his first sermon in the Deer Park at Sarnath. King Bimbisara offered a bamboo groove to Lord Buddha to establish the first forest monastery. Even when residences were offered to Lord Buddha and his followers in Rajgriha, they spent the three months long rain retreat in the forests. Throughout his travels, he stayed in various mango groves such as Pavarikambavana in Nalanda. The mango groves of Amrapli, Cunda and Jivaka are mentioned. In Kushinara, he passed away attaining *mahāparinirvāna* between a pair of sal trees.

Lord Buddha also had many encounters with animals. A symbolically important story is when Prince Siddhartha saved the sarus crane which was shot down by his cousin Devdutta. The sarus cranes, the world's tallest flying birds, are sacred to the people of the Indo-Gangetic plains. They still inhabit the wetlands around Lumbini and are being looked after by the Lumbini Crane Conservation Centre.

Sarus cranes in the circular pond

Buddhism and nature

There are different approaches within Buddhism on how to respond to nature. As Lambert Schmithausen, a professor of Buddhist Studies explains, there are two contradictory evaluations between the 'Pro-Civilization Strand' and the 'Hermit Strand'. The 'Pro-Civilization Strand' sees nature as something disagreeable and possibly full of danger. Human superiority is stressed and the city would be considered the ideal. On the other hand, the 'Hermit Strand' spends time in solitude in the wild. Here the positive value of animals and plants is understood and the notion that the ecosystem needs to be not only preserved but also restored if necessary is advocated. This strand of thought, together with the Buddhist ethos of not killing any living being and of compassion and benevolence, can be seen as the basis for various ecological movements (Schmithausen, 1990).

The concept of Buddha-nature began with the understanding that all sentient beings have a latent Buddha-hood. This understanding was further expanded especially in Far Eastern Buddhism to include plants, rocks, streams, mountains and the entire environment. This meant that non-sentient objects also have Buddha-nature and therefore need to be cared for.

> We classify other animals and living beings as nature, acting as if we ourselves are not part of it. Then we pose the question: 'How should we deal with Nature?' We should deal with nature the way we should deal with ourselves! We should not harm ourselves; we should not harm nature… Human beings and nature are inseparable (Nhát Hanh, 2008).

© Kai Weise

Turtles in Sacred pond

Native trees

Acacia catechu (Khayer)
Acacia rugata (Shikakai)
Adina cordifolia (Haldu)
Albizialebbek (Siris)
Albizziaprocera (Setosiris)
Alstoniascholaris (Chatiwan)
Annonareticulata (Ram
Phal, Sharipha)
Anthocephaluscadamba (Kadam)
Artocarpusintegrifolia Jack fruit
(RukhKatahar)
Artocarpuslakocha (Lakooch)
Azadirachtaindica (Neem)
Bassialatifolia (Mahua)
Bauhinia pupurea (Tanki)
Bombaxceiba Silk cotton tree (Simal)
Butea minor (Bhuletro)
Buteamonosperma, (Palans)
Carica papaya Papaya (Mewa)
Cassia fistula Indian laburnum
(Amaltas, Raja briksha)
Cedrelatoona (Toona)
Combretumroxburghii
Dalbergialatifolia (Sati sal)
Dalbergiasissoo (Sisau)
Dubangagrandiflora (PaniSaj)
Ficusbenghalensis (Bar)

Ficusbenjaa (Sami)
Ficusbenjamina (Sami)
Ficusglaberrima (Dumre)
Ficushederacea
Ficushispida (Khasreto)
Ficusoligodon
Ficusreligiosa (Pipal)
Ficussemicordata (Khanayo)
Fraxinus floribunda (Lankuri)
Gardenia jasminoides (Indra Kamal)
Litchi sinensis (Lichi)
Litseamonopetala (Kutmero)
Mallotusphilippensis (Rohini)
Mangiferaindica Mango (Amp)
Micheliachampaca (Champ)
Moringaoleifera (Sahijan)
Phyllanthusemblica (Amala)
Plumeriaacutifloria
Psidiunguajava Guava (Amba)
Shorearobusta (Sal, Sakhuwa)
Syzygiumjambos(Jamun)
Terminaliaalata (Saj)
Terminaliabelerica (Barro)
Terminaliachebula (Harro)
Terminaliamyriocarpa (Panisaj)
Zyzyhusmauritiana (Bayer)

Trees associated with Lord Buddha

Saracaashoka Ashoka tree
Shorearobusta Sal tree
Mangiferaindica Mango Tree
FicusPlaksha (Kavro Tree)

Ficusreligiosa Pipal tree
Ficusbengalensis Banyan Tree
Syzygiumcumini Java Plum
Date Palm (Tada)

Crops mentioned in Jataka

Oryza sativa Rice
Pennisetumtyphoides (Bajra)
Cicerarietinum Gram, Pigeon pea
Phaseolusaureus Mung or Golden Gram
Sesame indicum Sesamum
Brassica campsetris (Sarsyu)

Capsicum annum Chillie
Cuminumcyminum Cumin
Piper betel Betel leaves *(Pan)*
Areca catechu Areca nut *(Supari)*
Saccharumofficinarum Sugarcane *(Ukhu)*
Gossypiumarboreum Cotton *(Kapas)*

Flora

The habitat inside the Lumbini Garden is mainly composed of grassland (58.8 per cent), forest plantation (40 per cent) and open water bodies (1.5 per cent). The dominant grass species includes *imperatacylindrica, saccharummunja, phragmites* and *vetiver*. Along the two major rivers, Harhawa and Telar, there are many water bodies (ponds) in the depressed land. The major wetland plants include *vallisneria*, hydrilla, *potemogeton* (submerged), *nymphea, trapa, eichornia* (floating species) and *scirpus, eleochris, zizania, typha, polygonum, leersia, ipomea, oryzarufipogon* as emergent species.

Lord Buddha's life is directly related with trees. He was born under the Sal tree, he meditated under the *Pipal* tree, he attained enlightenment under a tree, first preached under a tree and the *mahāparinirvāna* took place under a tree. In ancient texts he is said to have slept under the *Neem* tree when he was ill.

The Lumbini area could be a significant place to develop as a natural garden, and an arboretum, which could become a conservation and demonstration area. Trees species that are native to the Terai and related to the culture should be represented here. The ponds surrounding the Sacred Garden could have wetland plants to add beauty to the landscape and attract wetland birds. The Holy lotus (*Nelumbonucifera*) is the flower that emerged under every step Lord Buddha took after his birth. The lotus flower has a high regard in Buddhism. Different species should dot the surface of ponds at the sacred site. The slopes of the circular levee should have a carpet of green grasses to prevent soil erosion. The establishment of a floating garden would attract birds and mammals.

Fauna

With the recreation of the wetlands and of the natural habitats inside the one by three mile Lumbini Project Area (LPA), birds and animals have been attracted, where nesting sites have been identified. The sites are being monitored and managed by the Lumbini Crane Conservation Centre, and are located in the following areas:

- Swamp areas beside the Vietnam Monastery and the Tara Monastery;
- North of the World Peace Stupa (Lumbini Crane Sanctuary);
- East of the World Peace Stupa (Lumbini Crane Sanctuary);
- Circular pond between Hokke Hotel and the Sri Lankan Pilgrims House.

The monitoring of the Sarus was initiated in 1988. Additionally there are about 100 flying bird species in and around a 10 km radius of the Lumbini Garden. A high count of eighty eight birds during the non-breeding season, along with twenty five nesting pairs, was recorded in 2005.

Blue bull antelopes have been colonizing the Lumbini garden area since the 1990s. Within a few years, the number rose to around 200 in 1995. It is reported that farmers, whose crop was being eaten, poisoned blue bulls between 1996 and 1998. In fact, up to seventy dead animals were recorded in the Lumbini area between the months of November and December 1997. The 1997 cold wave that hit the Terai was also a cause of the deaths of these animals. Under the aegis of the former King Mahendra Trust for Nature Conservation, five blue bulls were relocated to the Kusum Forest of Banke in 1998. In 2005, the number of blue bulls was around fifty.

Regarding other creatures, the Lumbini area has become a shelter for antelopes, which feed on the surrounding fields. Two pairs of Eurasian eagle owls regularly nest in the groves inside the garden. Similarly gray hornbills reside and nest inside the garden. The sick and old cattle that die inside the garden are cleaned by the endangered vulture, chiefly the white-rumped and slender-billed vultures.

Due to the increase in refuse, the number of crows is increasing and this constitutes a threat to other songbirds. They raid nests and eat eggs and chicks. They also mob other birds, occasionally bigger than them, including the Eurasian eagle owl.

Water and soil characteristics

Harhawa River: The catchment area of the Harhawa River is 21 km. The peak flood discharge is estimated at 160 cum/sec (in the Master Plan, the estimation of the maximum rainfall in 24 hours period is assumed to be 360 mm). The river basin is flooded several times each year and each flooding lasts four to five days. The river develops a typical floodplain of 100/120 metres in width – one to two metres below the surrounding grounds along the river course.

Telar River: The Telar flows east to the Sacred Garden. The name derives from the word 'tel', which means oil, since the water is thought to be oily in nature. This river is a landmark, mentioned by the Chinese travellers as flowing close to the birthplace of Lord Buddha.

The type of soil is clayish, permeability is very low, sodium level is high and the available phosphorus is very low. The soil is firm and the alkalinity level is high.

Tests of ground water samples

During April 1999, the Global Resources Institute and the International Buddhist Society sampled and tested the water from nine villages in the Lumbini area; collected the relevant data for project planning; discussed water and health conditions with the people of the villages; and made preliminary field tests of the solar disinfection technologies.

The survey indicated the importance and the primary role of water quality testing. In many cases, the simple identification of safe sources of drinking water will encourage the use of those sources rather than the unsafe ones. In a village having twenty five or thirty wells, there is some likelihood that at least a small number of these will be free of bacterial contamination. By making arrangements for the common use of these wells for drinking water, considerable reduction of water borne diseases can be expected. In many cases, it is likely that an improvement in water quality can be obtained by increasing well sanitation. Making sure that wells are properly grouted and sealed, that they have proper pads for the drainage of wastewater, and that only clean water is used for priming, are all simple and inexpensive methods for decreasing bacterial contamination.

Climatic conditions

Lumbini lies in the sub-tropical climatic zone, which experiences all four seasons. From March to May, there is a brief spring, which is followed by a long summer season, with high temperatures (up to 42.5°C), low humidity, thunder showers and heat waves that originate from the heat of the land.

Monsoon is the rainy season between mid-June and August. The maximum downpour recorded in 1999 was 223 mm of rain within 24 hours. September may remain wet because of the remaining monsoon clouds. October and November is the autumnal season, with a dry and warm climate in the daytime and cold temperatures at night. December, January and February are the winter seasons with foggy mornings and cold temperatures at night, which can drop to 5°C. Occasionally, cold spells occur throughout the Terai, with a dense layer of low fog. This fog hinders the penetration of sunlight and causes severe drops in the mean daytime temperature from 25° to 15°C. This may last for about a month and represents a threat to plants and animals and also poses a health hazard to human beings.

In Nepal, an atmospheric warming trend has been recorded since 1977. The annual average temperature rise ranges from 0.06°C to 0.12° C in the middle mountain and the Himalayan region, and of 0.03° C in the Siwalik and Terai regions.

Changing weather conditions in the past have had devastating effects on the area around Lumbini. 'It is also possible that some natural disasters, such as drought, famine, floods in the rainy season, or earthquakes caused people to abandon Lumbini' (Bidari, 2009, p. 30). The swampy ground further deteriorated the land and brought about diseases such as malaria making the area uninhabitable for humans. This took centuries to counter by draining the swamps and eradicating the malaria using large quantities of toxic chemicals and by turning the jungles into farmland.

Managing the natural resources and the environment

The people in areas adjoining Lumbini have huge aspirations and economic development expectations by taking advantage of its location. This has raised numerous environmental challenges that require mitigation and management. The airport in Bhairahawa and the adjoining villages, towns and cities could all be affected and in return, how they develop will affect Lumbini. Industries, commercial activities and even agricultural production tools and techniques must be looked at in terms of the long-term consequences on the local climate, hydrology, flora and fauna.

For over two millennia, people have come to Lumbini from all over the world. This can become an incentive for conservation of the natural environment of Lumbini, as well as a threat if not managed properly. The prediction of growing numbers of these visitors mean, some forecasting will have to be made so that management can become proactive instead of reactive. Being able to influence the behaviour of the visitors will be as important as the ability to manage the resources. Lumbini also has the potential to inspire conservation globally and locally.

The link between the birth and life of Siddhartha Gautama and the natural environment is greatly emphasized in Buddhist literature and iconography. Images of the birth of Lord Buddha show Mayadevi supporting herself on a tree. The stories and parables told of the Lord Buddha are often presented with animal protagonists. In the Jantaka tales, Buddhist ethical teachings are told by the Lord Buddha in various incarnations in human and animal form. The sarus crane, which is mentioned in the stories of young Siddhartha, still migrate through Lumbini and roost in the area. This close link between Buddhism and the environment can be an inspiration to develop closer links and respect for the environment around Lumbini.

Since the eradication of malaria from the Terai there has been massive migration of hill people into the settlements in plains. Development pressures and over-extraction of natural resources is wreaking havoc on the environment. Nepal has been identified as one of the most vulnerable countries to the effects of climate change. In the past, climate change has devastated this region. Today we will have to find means of mitigating the impact through improving the understanding and amity to the environment.

It is also necessary to look at the state of natural resources in the wider region of the three districts in the region, namely, Kapilvastu, Rupandehi and Nawalparasi. For example the removal and sale of gravel and sand from the rivers and watershed areas could pose an environmental challenge and threat to Lumbini and the other historical sites related to the birth and life of Lord Buddha. In the past, when mining was only for domestic use, the volume was insignificant. Now there is an unabated demand in Nepal and in India for these natural resources. Buildings, roads canals and other infrastructure have put a huge demand and offer an attractive price on gravel and sand. Agricultural practices, the crops grown, as well as the methods utilized could affect the Lumbini area as well. The ancient ways of life are part and parcel of the heritage of Lumbini.

The Lumbini Crane Conservation Centre (LCCC) has a 50 year lease agreement to manage 100 hectares as a sarus crane sanctuary on the northern block of the Lumbini Project Area. Similarly, International Union for Conservation of Nature (IUCN Nepal), the Tourism and Rural Poverty Alleviation Project of UNDP, the Department for International Development (DFID) and SNV Netherlands Development Organization have helped to protect wetlands and manage some of the adverse impacts such as waste and helped local communities with the adoption of renewable and clean energy sources such as bio-gas. The 20-plus monasteries that have been built in Lumbini by the various Buddhist groups representing different countries have added both greenery and water bodies that have attracted more birds. This factor, combined with a more peaceful environment, has improved the breeding grounds for different species of birds.

Conservation and natural resources management efforts in Nepal over the past decades have had to evolve with the changing political scenario in the country. The protection of the environment can only realistically take place with the participation of local inhabitants. Local villagers and farmers need to work with the members of green clubs at local schools and local guides need training to interpret the importance of Lumbini and the surrounding environment. A broad citizen base of support is needed for the conservation of Lumbini and its surrounding areas.

It was suggested that, in Lumbini visitors must be informed about the do's and don'ts and be properly briefed before they proceed along the central canal to the Sacred Garden. Alternative transport in the form of electric vehicles can be provided for the physically challenged and senior citizens. Plastic bags, disposable water bottles and other waste should be discouraged from being brought to the site. Waste disposal measures, such as reed-bed waste water treatment and composting can also be introduced. To further protect the site, visitors can be provided with cloth shoe covers or straw shoes. The visitors and pilgrims can also be educated to be conservation allies and help create a new ethos for a zero footprint on the local ecology, while maximizing their contribution to the local economy.

Vegetation outside the circular levee, Scared Garden

Environmental Impact Assessment of industrial development around Lumbini

The Industrial Promotion Board under the Ministry of Industry of the Government of Nepal established a Lumbini Protected Zone (LPZ) in 2009 and carbon-emitting industries would not be allowed to operate in the LPZ. The LPZ is an area within a 15 km aerial distance from the north, east and west boundaries of the Lumbini Project Area (the one by three square mile area) and towards the south up to the Indian border. It covers an area of about 828 sq km, including 44 VDCs in Rupandehi District and 25 VDCs in Kapilavastu District.

Despite the government decision, a rapid and uncontrolled growth of carbon emitting industries within the LPZ still threatens the Lumbini World Heritage Property. The expansion of the carbon emission industries causes numerous problems such as threatening the biodiversity, creating a health hazard to the locals and affecting archaeological vestiges.

Therefore, an environmental impact assessment (EIA) of the industrial development around Lumbini was carried out by IUCN Nepal as requested by UNESCO in August 2011. This EIA study was undertaken with funding from the Paris based non-governmental organization the 'Oriental Cultural Heritage Sites Protection Alliance'.

The EIA conducted by IUCN Nepal identified fifty-seven industries in the region. Of these industries, fifteen were identified as major industries in terms of their production processes and pollutant emissions. The study has developed concise zoning guidelines and prepared an environmental plan and monitoring strategy to reduce the impact of industrial activities in the area.

The study revealed that industries prefer this region because of the availability of cheap labour, water and easy road access to the border. They are also provided with preferential access to existing infrastructure such as an electricity supply and paved roads.

Most of the industries operating in the Lumbini Road Industrial Corridor do not conform to the Environment Protection Act (EPA) and related environmental guidelines. This has created an impact on the environment, flora, fauna and the local community, as well as on the health of the workers. The condition of the surface and groundwater quality varies from medium to bad. The study found that the soil is slightly alkaline; however, no toxicity was found. The organic matter in the soil was lower than the accepted standard and this indicates that the soil is affected by fugitive effluent from cement factories.

The study has proposed five zones within the LPZ, each with a definite degree of environmental protection. Mitigation measures for the reduction of air, water, noise, and soil pollution were identified, along with environmental management plans and compliances. The auditing frameworks were arranged to review the environmental impacts in the future. The existing carbon emitting industries need to be shifted from the LPZ within a certain period for the long-term development of Lumbini. The government needs to consider providing compensation and alternatives to the owners of industries. This can be implemented through a regional plan which develops the surrounding region and keeps the conservation of cultural heritage a priority.

Polluting industries that impact Lumbini, taken in 2011

© Kai Wei

Perception Seven

Balancing competing requirements of faith and preservation

The site must cater to the very varied needs of different visitor groups, mainly pilgrims and tourists, who carry out a variety of activities. These include religious deeds such as making offerings, burning incense, etc. However related activities and required facilities might create conflict between the various groups of visitors (conflicting activities within the same area by both pilgrims and tourists) and impact on the archaeological remains and sanctity, authenticity and integrity of the site.

Content

Analysis of visitors. Inner Sacred Garden. Outer Sacred Garden. Balancing tourism and preservation.

References

This chapter is based on contributions by Sayalay Bhaddamanika, with input from Lisa Choegyal.

Analysis of visitors

The dual nature of Lumbini as a place of pilgrimage and an archaeological site attracts different types of visitors, including Buddhist pilgrims, non-Buddhist pilgrims, members of resident Buddhist communities and tourists. Other users of the site include special guests, site management staff, media, security personnel, etc.

Visitors to the inner and outer Sacred Garden carry out numerous activities and they perform these with great reverence to the site testifying to the value of the World Heritage Property. But these same activities often have an impact on the elements and attributes that constitute the Outstanding Universal Value of the World Heritage Property. The various religious communities, the tourists and those, who are managing the site, place wide ranging demands on the site. The activities and needs of the visitors must be considered in any planning for the preservation and presentation of the Sacred Garden and they need to be classified, depending on their impact on the sanctity and integrity of the site.

The main archaeological artefacts, which are highly revered by visitors, are located in the inner Sacred Garden, where most of the activities are concentrated. The outer Sacred Garden surrounding the main site is considered to be a protective area.

Sacred pond and remains of ancient stupas

Inner Sacred Garden

The inner Sacred Garden as Lumbini's most sacred area is at the heart of the Kenzo Tange Master Plan and the core zone of the World Heritage Property. It hosts the main pilgrimage structures of high archaeological and religious value and is characterized by a peaceful atmosphere inspiring a sense of serene faith and tranquillity.

Visitors come to Lumbini's core area to perform different activities. Among them, the pilgrims represent the most important visitor group. Often wearing distinctive clothes, they pay homage to Lord Buddha by meditating, chanting religious stanzas, reciting holy texts and worshiping the archaeological remains that mark his birthplace. In addition, they perform a variety of other activities. The following list details some of these.

Pilgrims gather throughout the year to celebrate specific ceremonies such as:
- Conducting prayer programmes led by a monastic community on full moon days and other significant religious occasions;
- Uniting with Buddhist devotees and the monastic communities for special religious occasions;
- Monk ordinations;
- Novice initiations.

Pilgrims carry out actions that could conflict with other visitors such as:
- Chanting religious stanzas;
- Giving and listening to talks about Lord Buddha and the history of Lumbini;
- Meditating;
- Circumambulating and prostrating.

Most visitors bring offerings to the site and perform activities such as:
- Lighting candles and incense;
- Offering oil lamps;
- Offering butter lamps;
- Offering monetary donations;
- Offering milk;

- Offering scented water;
- Hanging lines of Tibetan prayer flags;
- Placing flags on the fence surrounding the Ashoka Pillar;
- Placing robes on the grille around the Ashoka Pillar;
- Offering coins to the Ashoka Pillar;
- Offering hair to the Ashoka Pillar;
- Gilding the archaeological monuments;
- Smearing red powder on the archaeological remains.

Activities, which can have a direct impact on archaeological vestiges, include:
- Stepping on the ancient monuments;
- Sitting and relaxing on the archaeological remains;
- Splashing milk onto the Ashoka Pillar;
- Splashing perfumed water on the Ashoka Pillar;
- Throwing coins at the Ashoka Pillar;
- Lighting candles and burning incense very close to the ancient monuments;
- Removing ancient bricks from the archaeological remains inside the Mayadevi Temple;
- Removing soil from the base of the ancient monuments.

Other activities conflict with the sanctity of the site or may even be illegal such as:
- Stealing donations from donation boxes;
- Selling souvenirs in the vicinity of Lord Buddha's birthplace;
- Operating food and snack stalls at the entrance to the main sacred area;
- The regular presence of false monastics.

Most of these activities have subtle spiritual value, but some of them negatively impact on the site's sanctity and peace, generate conflict with other visitors or represent threats to the preservation of the monuments Finding the right balance between these aspects is a major planning and management challenge.

Some activities carried out by visitors have a long-term negative impact on the archaeological values of the site, such as throwing coins at the Ashoka Pillar, gilding archaeological remains with gold leaves, splashing milk and chemical based perfumed-water on monuments. Pilgrims are also illicitly taking brick pieces from the monuments, while accessing the place where the Marker Stone has been placed. Other activities have caused environmental pollution, e.g. of the *Pushkarini* Pond (Sacred Pond) and of the artificial water bodies around the Sacred Garden.

According to the Kenzo Tange Master Plan, the Sacred Garden around the main archaeological remains should be an area with minimum infrastructure. All modern structures within this area were to be removed and only historically authenticated remains were to be maintained. However, this vision conflicts with the basic requirement of the visitors such as the need for toilets, drinking fountains and rest areas. There is also a lack of space to perform religious activities required by the different Buddhist traditions. For example, there are no other images than the Nativity Sculpture presenting Mayadevi with the baby Siddhartha. However, not all Buddhist traditions pray to Mayadevi; some of them pay obeisance to statues of Lord Buddha. Presently, the two monasteries located within the Sacred Garden, the Nepal Buddha Vihar and the Dharma Swami Maharaja Buddha Vihar, provide solace to accommodate some of these religious practices.

Several proposals have been made to reduce the negative impact of visitors on the site and to improve the balance between heritage protection and the quality of experience of the pilgrims. They include:

a) Regular monitoring of the activities of the visitors;
b) Providing information on the excavated archaeological remains;
c) Establishing signboards to request decent physical and verbal behaviour within the Sacred Garden;
d) Introducing measures to reduce noise pollution, e.g. pilgrimage groups need to be encouraged to refrain from the use of loudspeakers;
e) Raising visitors' awareness about the need to protect and preserve the environment;
f) Creating serene meditation spots for pilgrims seeking solitude.

Outer Sacred Garden

The outer Sacred Garden functions as a buffer zone of the inner Sacred Garden. The main access to the Sacred Garden is from the north along the central canal. However, other gates are also being used to access the inner Sacred Garden, such as the east gate, the south-west gate, through the wooded area, which is used mostly by people from the surrounding villages and the western gates, which are presently closed to prevent grazing cattle from entering.

In the outer Sacred Garden, which has not been used for any particular purpose, the many activities that could have an impact on its environment and its sanctity are of great concern. These activities include fishing and fish-trapping by damming rain water drains, poaching endangered animals such as blue bulls and pythons and the illegal trading of endangered bird species. Other harmful activities include logging and cutting trees for firewood. Other actions that have an impact on the environment are cattle grazing, illegal logging, and the dumping of waste and soil from excavations in various parts of the natural landscape.

The improvement and protection of the natural environment, which is largely a forested area, would create the appropriate setting to encase the birthplace of Lord Buddha. A quiet, clean and harmonious surrounding would greatly enhance and protect the sacredness of the main archaeological site.

Good examples are the tree planting projects and the plantation of flowering shrubs along the eastern access road to the entrance of the inner Sacred Garden area and along some sections of the circular levee.

The outer Sacred Garden has been neglected in the past and there are no guidelines for its development and use. To protect this area it is essential that environmental issues become the concern of all stakeholders, especially the local people who reside in the surrounding communities.

There are several issues that should be addressed in guidelines for the development and use of the outer Sacred Garden. For example, regular maintenance is required of the circular levee road which connects visitors to the different components of the Master Plan area. The outer Sacred

Garden must become a bird sanctuary especially for endangered bird species. Trails need to be provided for bird-watching. Regulations need to be enacted to protect avian and aquatic species. Tree planting programmes need to be enhanced. Natural meditation areas should be created in the cool and peaceful wooded areas.

Migratory birds in the circular pond

Balancing tourism and preservation

Many of the above issues require a wider tourism planning taking such issues as access, tourism patterns and visitor spending into account. In addition to physical amenities, the 'software' of visitor facilities is urgently required such as training, guiding and interpretation. These can be of a scale and style to encourage the involvement of local people and thus contributing to improving their livelihood.

Conflicting use by pilgrims and tourists is a visitor management issue that is familiar and common in many sites. Various visitor activities need to be addressed and solved with a spectrum of appropriate visitor management mechanisms. Conflicts between visitor segments are only one of a range of issues that need to be considered in overall visitor planning.

The first principal is that visitor activities must not damage the physical fabric nor compromise the spiritual values, sanctity and integrity of the site. There are many examples across Asia in which tourism and conservation can reinforce each other and are not in conflict. The key is control and management and partnerships amongst the stakeholders. The monastery managers need to be engaged and can play an important role in implementing solutions. Likewise, food stalls, local produce, souvenirs and curio shops provide a service for visitors and a means of delivering tourism benefits to the local community. Consequently, they should be controlled and managed, but not stopped.

There are some subtle activities that are very much related to the spiritual values and some could lead to potential conflicts among stakeholder groups. These have to be managed carefully by building consensus among all stakeholders and finding constructive ways to lessen those conflicts. Based on the various forms of visitor activities, such findings are alarming and cause conflicts, especially in the inner Sacred Garden where significant archaeological values exist. Regular monitoring of threats to the Outstanding Universal Value (OUV) and addressing them should be given priority. Clear and effective guidelines for all visitors to the site needs to be formulated and implemented.

It is important to balance the competing requirements of faith and conservation. These two aspects can be brought together to lay the foundation for dialogue that gives equal weight to the beliefs and faith of the spiritual community and the interests and needs of conservation. It is important to stress that the use of the site, including by pilgrims, could have a negative impact on both values if it involves alteration of the tangible features that represent those values. For this reason, the use of the site must reflect an agreed vision of the concerned stakeholders based on the OUV of the site. Participation by all stakeholders in workshops that strengthen knowledge about the protection of tangible values of the site is an important activity for long-term preservation of the site. The staging of meetings and workshops to raise awareness and provide heritage education about the protection and development of Lumbini will help protect this World Heritage Property.

Some of the visitors' activities that can be categorized as negative are difficult to address as such because they are conducted in the sense of spirituality and may seem innocent. However, they can become threats to the archaeological values from a conservation point of view.

> The immediate surroundings of the Marker Stone are dirty because of the pilgrim's offerings and the presence of mice. The Nativity Sculpture seems to be well preserved, due to the efficacy of the treatments performed last year and the reduced quantity of offerings that have accumulated at the base of the sculpture. The Ashoka Pillar is in general well preserved but the inscription is affected by a lightening of the sandstone around some of the letters, while the column shows draining of milk and other liquids in several places interspersed as offering [s] (Meucci, 2012, p. 3).

In order to preserve the OUV of the site, all concerned stakeholders will have to build bridges and work with consideration to accommodate the views of all interested parties. While preserving the ancient monuments at the site, environmental protection of the area also needs to be taken seriously. Since the life of Lord Buddha is very much connected to nature, it is of utmost importance to address the issues of potential threats to the ecosystem of the site.

© Kai Weise

Perception Eight

Peace and tranquillity. What visitors expect from the Sacred Garden

What do pilgrims, tourists, managers, experts and those who visit Lumbini from the surrounding villages, expect from the Sacred Garden? Almost all of these individual or collective expectations are based on some or all of the issues raised in the previous chapters and how these issues are addressed to create a harmonious and sacred place. The expectations of the visitors will be fulfilled by the resolution of these issues and the cumulative impression created to express the character of the site.

Content

Visions of peace and serenity. Revealing the expectations.

References

This chapter is based on contributions by Gyanin Rai and Basanta Bidari. Reference has also been attributed to contributions by Robin Coningham and Christoph Cüppers.

Visions of peace and serenity

As described in the previous chapters, Lumbini is not only a pilgrimage site for Buddhists but it is also a symbolic place for people, who wish to promote peace throughout the world. The site is ideal for practitioners of meditation; fascinating for researchers and journalists; a challenge for architects and conservationists; and a source of livelihood for the local people. They all have different interests in the site, but they all expect Lumbini to be developed as a sacred place for those who believe in peace and are in search of peace.

Everybody would like to see Lumbini as a peaceful and tranquil place. There is however a difference in the way how people feel peace and how they understand a place to be tranquil. Obviously, the reason for their visit to Lumbini determines their expectation. Pilgrims want Lumbini to be a holy place and are satisfied when a place for worship is made available and properly managed. Those who come to Lumbini to meditate, seek a suitable place to meditate. Visitors such as researchers, journalists and photographers would like to have more information on the historical aspect of the site with more signage and a clean environment.

The following statement by one visitor expresses the opinion of many: 'Lumbini is an open school, where every visitor, a pilgrim, meditation practitioner, tourist, researcher, or of any profession, can get satisfaction by realizing and experiencing peace.'

This testimony is one among those that were collected towards the end of 2010, when a series of interviews were carried out to develop a better understanding of what visitors expect when they come to Lumbini.

The interviews aimed at identifying the components that would make the Sacred Garden the peaceful and tranquil place that the visitors expect to find when they come to Lumbini. The replies clearly indicate that the main expectation that visitors have from the Sacred Garden is that of a place for meditation, spiritual nourishment and contemplation. For all of them, Lumbini with its bearing of ancient history, knowledge and inspiration, is a holy place reflecting the importance as the place where Lord Buddha took his first steps on earth. Most visitors expressed the view that they would like Lumbini to be enhanced with the creation of a natural setting with gardens and large trees spread over the wider surrounding area in the spirit of the Kenzo Tange Master Plan.

Indeed, many visitors believe that the improvement of the physical setting of the Sacred Garden will help develop Lumbini in a sustainable way. For example, establishing gardens with indigenous plants would not only enhance greenery but also help reduce pollution, provide a habitat for wild animals, offer a suitable environment for meditation practitioners, control noise and protect the Sacred Garden from industrial pollution.

Many visitors also expect better information. They deplore a lack of signage systems and information boards particularly on Lord Buddha's life. They also would like to see display boards mentioning behavioural guidelines that should be respected to maintain the Sacred Garden as a place of peace and tranquillity, for example by restricting drinking, eating and smoking.

A majority of the visitors wish that the archaeological remains are adequately protected. They believe for example that it would be important to fence the most important remains without obstructing their visibility.

Visitors also made suggestions for realizing their expectations. They can be summarized under six broad categories:

1. A precondition for attaining the expectations is effective management and administration of the site.
2. A key issue is that archaeological values of the site need to be protected.
3. To increase awareness and to educate the visitor, information must be provided in various forms along with improved signage.
4. Partnerships with stakeholders and development agencies are required.
5. Strict guidelines and controls on behaviour within the Sacred Garden are essential to ensure the maintenance of a sacred, serene and harmonious environment.
6. The highest quality must be maintained for all interventions that are carried out within the Sacred Garden.

Revealing the expectations

The interviewees were asked to explain in one sentence their expectations of the Sacred Garden. They responses were in general very articulated. For example, some expect the Sacred Garden to be conserved and managed, including all the archaeological remains and monuments. They said that the living traditions should be taken into consideration in this context. The 'proof' of the birthplace of Lord Buddha should also be protected. The Sacred Garden with its combination of natural, archaeological and ritual elements should form a coherent and unified space, said others. Lumbini should be protected as a sacred place with clarity, authenticity and quality. Many agreed that the Kenzo Tange Master Plan should be completed in keeping with its spirit and vision – but with all the necessary 21st century updates.

As stated earlier, the most common expectation was that the Sacred Garden must be a quiet, tranquil, beautiful and peaceful place, a pleasure for visitors. It must be clean and without pollution. The authorities must manage and preserve its archaeological monuments and protect its authenticity as the birthplace of Lord Buddha. The Sacred Garden must have a spiritual and holy environment and must be a place of prayer, religious inspiration, faith, meditation, contemplation and reflection. Another common expectation that was expressed in the interviews is that the Garden must also be a place of knowledge and learning and for spreading peace throughout the world.

© Kai Weise

Monks gathering in Lumbini

Examples of comments:

- A great reflection place within a historically authentic setting.
- Opportunity to discover the role to the site on the development of Buddhism.
- A quiet place for reflection and appreciation of the landscape and monuments.
- Place that inspires one to walk on the path of Buddha.
- A peaceful space accessible to all.
- Quiet, clean, beautiful, pollution-free and a place of religious inspiration.
- Buddhist faith, preserving archaeological ruins and place of peace.
- To provide an atmosphere that fosters spiritual nourishment.
- To experience the ancient history and holiness of the Lord Buddha's place of birth.
- A peaceful and tranquil place where one can contemplate the birth and life of Sakya Sakyamuni Buddha.
- It should be a place of contemplation and silence set in nature.
- Peaceful area with a large tree, smaller and less spread out.
- Power / Energy / Peace / Holy.
- Peaceful place, beautiful garden and well managed site.
- A peaceful spot, where people are practicing meditation.
- Silence, beauty, energy and spirituality.
- Peace, quiet and mystic.
- It is very special and beautiful, peaceful and a highlight to see.
- A peaceful, clean and uplifting peace.
- A pleasant quiet place for meditation and prayer.
- Quiet, peaceful garden.
- History and knowledge.
- Peaceful, no noise pollution.
- Spiritual environment/ peaceful / No pollution.
- I did not have any expectations, but it is very beautiful.

Appearance

The interviewed visitors were asked to formulate their expectations on the visual characteristics of the Sacred Garden and specific actions that are required to better fulfil these expectations. The component most mentioned was the improvement of the gardens. This would include planting of trees and improving the overall environment with greenery. The comments on structures can be divided into the improvement of existing structures and removal of structures. Comments were made on improving the Mayadevi Temple (or removing it) and the walkways, providing toilets and removing the surrounding fencing.

Examples of comments:
- Maintain greenery, beautiful green plants, lot of flowers and trees.
- Remove Mayadevi Temple — replace with architecture more appropriate to the character of the Sacred Garden.
- Visual and processional characteristics that are the essence of the Tange plan must be understood by all stakeholders so that the Tange vision guides all improvement plans.
- Do not change visual and processional characteristics of Tange plan.
- Ideally more light in the Mayadevi Temple complex.
- Regarding building structures: uncover and preserve, don't create.
- More beautiful Mayadevi temple building.
- Some visuals about the birth of Buddha and the life he spent in this area.

Under the Bodhi tree

Management

The comments on management were mainly in respect to inappropriate activities, but also on the need to improve facilities. Visitors expect a better management of local festivals and curio shops. Eating, drinking and smoking should not be allowed. The guards should not be armed. Interpretation should be provided to explain the site. Cleanliness must be improved. This would include waste management in the Sacred Garden, especially next to the Ashoka Pillar. The pond should also be kept clean. The archaeological remains must be conserved, further excavations carried out and the essence of Kenzo Tange Master Plan implemented.

All management related suggestions are linked to the expectations of the visitors that the site reflects a spiritual atmosphere that is conducive to meditation.

Examples of comments:
- Maybe a bit cleaner (it is clean but as a sacred place, it should be without any litter and impeccably clean).
- During the day time, you should be able to see greenery all around you.
- Well management track /road and big gate, path for walkers.
- Food, drinks, smoking should not be allowed.
- Plants, maybe animal / deer.
- Garbage management.
- Manage local festivals.Manage curio shops.
- Remove weapons holder security.
- Manage shoes / sleeper rack.
- Fence on archaeological remains.
- Develop spirituality.
- Carry out more archaeological diggings to place the historic value of this place.
- Area for prayers.
- Maybe few more visualizations, about how it used to look and work.
- More diverse plants and trees, native to the area.

Infrastructure

The interviewed visitors were asked to formulate their expectations on the infrastructure of Lumbini and specific actions that are required to better fulfil these expectations. The most important requirement was the construction of toilet facilities. It was also suggested that a visitor centre be established with further facilities, including an information booth, restaurants, canteen, shops and parking. The existing shops and stalls need to be relocated. Another important requirement is to improve the footpath, especially around the ancient monuments, but also through the green areas. Meditation areas along with drinking water need to be provided in strategic locations.

Examples of comments:
- Stalls and shops should be moved outside of the Master Plan area or to the cultural centre.
- It shouldn't cost money to enter the Sacred Garden.
- More and better and cleaner toilets.
- Complete road system inside the Master Plan area.
- At the entrance to the complex there is a need for a visitor centre with a pilgrim information booth, adequate parking, visitor facilities (toilet, restaurant, shops).
- Need for tourist facilities (toilets, stand selling water/drinks) at strategic points within Master Plan area.
- Need adequate crowd control measures to decongest Sacred Garden at peak pilgrimage times.
- Some interaction spots, boards with detailed information about the place, history and importance and about Buddhism.
- Pathways through trees/prayer flags.
- Meditation cushions.
- Water and sanitation.
- Resting chairs.
- Welcome gate.
- Sufficient footpath.
- Buddhist courses for non-Buddhists.
- Vendors/souvenir/book stall should be relocated from existing position, so as to keep the passage wide open.

- Seating benches may be placed in and around Mayadevi Temple, Ashoka Pillar and Garden area.
- Drinking water fountain (may be 2 / 3, if placed at suitable location, will be a great relief to pilgrims.
- Praying/meditation spot.
- Toilet.
- Canteen.
- Parking.
- Spiritual activities.
- Place for meditation.
- Knowledgeable guide.
- Improve the footpaths, it may be more logical.
- Better access to Marker Stone and Nativity Sculpture.
- Few signs near the stupa, ruins.
- Easy walk around the ruins to see all ancient monuments.
- Small place for meditation.
- Keep the entire ground silent.
- Keep very natural.
- Maps with current status (Not Master Plan from the 1970s).

Visitors to the Nativity Statue

Function

As regards to expectations on the functions and activities in Lumbini and specific actions that are required to better fulfil these expectations, visitors interviewed considered meditation including sitting quietly, contemplating and praying as the main function. Further activities that were listed include relaxation, reading and visiting the archaeological sites. Activities such as having picnics, running, shouting and hanging banners should take place outside the Sacred Garden.

Examples of comments:

- Allow/encourage meditation practice, religious rituals/puja (circumambulation, chanting, etc.).
- Picnics should take place outside the Sacred Garden area.
- Relate to the Buddha's life through viewing archaeological remains.
- Please change architecture of Mayadevi Temple.
- It is always going to be difficult to meet everyone's expectations. Some will wish to visit as tourists; some will come for purely educational visits, some due to curiosity, whilst others wish to visit as a pilgrimage and don't wish to be treated as tourists. I am definitely in the latter category. I hope that somehow, quiet parts of the garden can be maintained for quiet contemplation, prayer and meditation.
- When I first visited on January 1, 2003, I was disappointed. Here was such a wonderfully auspicious place for one of the great religions of the world (my religion), and yet it felt more like an archaeological site for tourists. I am very, very happy to say that I think fantastic progress has been made since that time. PLEASE endeavour to make sure that it is first and foremost a site of pilgrimage.
- People running around, shouting, putting up huge banners in front of the pillar, having picnics, etc., takes away the atmosphere. I have no great suggestions, apart perhaps of ensuring that there are other attractive areas close to the main garden where people can relax, laugh, chat, eat, but without disturbing the pilgrimage area.
- Place of worship, meditation, unity with nature.
- Informative spot on Buddhism, its history and values, etc.
- Meditation and rest for the mind.

- Photography/read books.
- Walking/sitting/quiet.
- Learn something/meditation.
- Water music, peace music.
- Maintaining the existing peace and realize the words/statements of Buddha.
- Information desk for those who want more info about this place.
- Appreciate Buddhist temples for what they offer to inspire visitors.
- In my case, motivation to practice Dharma.
- Volunteering to do more for the pilgrims.
- Here is very nice and great with holy Lord Buddha, people improve much from this place.
- Place to get peace, spiritual vibration.
- Feeling peace by heart.
- Maybe one *gompa* for meditation.
- Heavily religious oriented.
- Dress for visitors should be white or yellow.
- Place of beauty.
- Place of silence.
- Place and space to feel the energy.
- Respect Buddha and more trees, flowers.
- Seating under shade and feel peace.

Discourse in the Sacred Garden

In summary, the expectations of Lumbini, as expressed by the survey of visitors, provides a broad image for the Sacred Garden. The site must be peaceful, quiet and harmonious with nature to allow for meditation and contemplation. It must preserve the archaeological testimony to the long history of Lumbini and be presented to visitors in a meaningful manner. To achieve this, the site must be managed properly to ensure the implementation of a code of conduct to protect the site's sacredness. This would also require the improvement of the environment, the removal of inappropriate structures and the relocation of some activities. The improvement of infrastructure focuses especially on providing toilets and drinking water.

Most of the visitors expect the Sacred Garden to be managed in a way in which the beauty of the place is enhanced and its peaceful and sacred atmosphere maintained. Management activities must cater to a great variety of views from a wide range of stakeholders.

More specifically, the visitors recommend the plantation of native species of trees to improve the environment. To ensure a clean environment, a better waste management system is required. Fences should be built only where they are absolutely necessary. Better information needs to be provided through various means such as signage, information boards and leaflets.

The survey also revealed differences between the expectations of visitors from abroad and those of the people from the local communities. The latter expect that they can carry out their own rituals, partake in general activities and profit from the Sacred Garden and use the space also for recreational activities. The participation of the local communities in the various tasks of ensuring the protection and sanctity of the site is considered by many interviewees as essential. The involvement of the community can produce mutual benefits for both the community and Lumbini.

© Kai Weise

Conclusion

Many international experts' reports, such as those of the joint missions of UNESCO and ICOMOS, state a lack of a vision for the Sacred Garden that would guide all conservation and management policies in Lumbini. This study of eight perceptions of the Sacred Garden of Lumbini defines this vision and provides a multifarious understanding of the Sacred Garden.

The perceptions compiled in this publication and, in the last chapter on the expectations of the visitors from the Sacred Garden represent the viewpoints and sentiments of a great variety of individuals and communities, who consider themselves stakeholders of Lumbini. They provide a complex, mosaic-like image of the Sacred Garden of Lumbini and make us better understand how people have seen Lumbini through the centuries and what they expect and experience when visiting the sacred place today.

These perceptions have been partially verified through the archaeological research that has been carried out in Lumbini over the past decades. The findings provide us with an account of the physical traces that contribute to the better understanding of early developments and events on the site.

Further layers of perceptions were added with the development of the Kenzo Tange Master Plan for Lumbini and the inscription of the property in the World Heritage List, which puts emphasis on the conservation of the archaeological site while taking into account the environment and the visitors.

No doubt, all these perceptions, as varied as they may be, contribute to a more comprehensive and inclusive interpretation of Lumbini. However, for the management of the site, a consensus is needed on how to relate and respect the viewpoints and sentiments of Lumbini's stakeholders. Each perception helps build on the understanding of the other perceptions. The archaeologist must understand the pilgrim; the historian the monk; the environmentalist the local farmer. It is this dialogue that will defuse conflicts. Each person that lays claim to Lumbini provides a unique value element to the heritage property. At the same time, each person interested in Lumbini must also accept all others and ensure that all actions and expectations take into account the sustainability of the heritage as something that we inherit from past generations, that is of great value to us and is worthy of preservation for the future.

Annexes

Conservation and development guidelines

The guidelines for the physical plan of the Sacred Garden of Lumbini were prepared in cooperation with all relevant authorities, stakeholders and experts.

Part A. Guidelines to protect the World Heritage Property and its Outstanding Universal Value

1   *Safeguard the attributes that convey the Outstanding Universal Value of the property*
The Outstanding Universal Value (OUV) of the property will be safeguarded, by managing the attributes that convey OUV and ensuring the authenticity and integrity of the property. The highest level of national and international protection shall be provided for the World Heritage Property.

2   *Extent of World Heritage boundary*
The existing World Heritage boundary is to be extended to cover the entire Inner Sacred Garden and all archaeological sites within the entire Sacred Garden area and planning will be carried out taking this into consideration.

3   *Extent of Buffer Zone to World Heritage and its protection*
The Buffer Zone to the World Heritage Property is to be extended to encompass the entire Outer Sacred Garden and planning will be carried out taking this into consideration.

4   *Protection through 'Zones of Influence'*
The 'Zone of Influence' will be considered as the Lumbini Development Area of five by five miles as per Kenzo Tange's Master Plan and this area will be planned and the required legislation put into place to ensure appropriate development that does not impact the integrity of the World Heritage Property in any manner such as the degradation of archaeological material through pollution.

5   *Provisions for Serial Nomination*
Provisions shall be made to allow for extension of the property to include further Buddhist sites in the districts of Kapilbastu, Rupandehi and Nawalparasi in the form of a serial nomination.

6   *The site manager of the World Heritage property*
The site manager shall be the Lumbini Development Trust, with the specific responsibility to coordinate all affairs related to managing, monitoring and reporting on the World Heritage Property.

7   *Heritage Impact Assessment*
All development activities that are undertaken within the Sacred Garden area shall have to pass a Heritage Impact Assessment.

Part B. Guidelines to address the Kenzo Tange Master Plan

8   Consideration of the atmosphere in the Sacred Garden
The Sacred Garden is to have an atmosphere of tranquillity, universality and clarity.

9   Boundaries of Sacred Garden as defined in Kenzo Tange's Master Plan
The Sacred Garden is to be defined as per the area indicated in Kenzo Tange's Master Plan (1600 x 1360 metres)

10   Consideration of the provisions for roads within Inner Sacred Garden
The concept of an abstract grid system of access roads as per the Kenzo Tange Master Plan can be considered in areas where there are clearly no potential archaeological sites, however with appropriate paving materials.

11   Consideration of the provisions for the archaeological site
The provisions defined in Kenzo Tange's Master Plan for the archaeological site shall be taken as the basis for all planning done within the Sacred Garden. However no activities shall be allowed that cause any kind of damage or affects the archaeological vestiges.

12   Consideration of the approach to the Sacred Garden
The main approach to the Sacred Garden for visitors will be from the north.

13   Consideration of controlling flooding
The planning of the Sacred Garden will ensure that flooding and ground water table is controlled to safeguard the archaeological vestiges.

14   Consideration of existing and new structures within the Sacred Garden
All planning in respect to existing structures and new structures within the Sacred Garden shall follow the provisions in Kenzo Tange Master Plan, however provide basic reversible facilities.

Part C. Guidelines to ensure an appropriate and sustainable environment

15   Ensuring an appropriate natural setting within the Sacred Garden
The natural setting within the Sacred Garden shall take into account the spiritual context of the birthplace of Lord Buddha as a place of pilgrimage.

16   Ensuring the protection of wildlife and their habitat around the Sacred Garden
Wildlife and their natural habitat will be strictly protected in the Sacred Garden, in Kenzo Tange's Master Plan area, as well as the surrounding region.

17   Ensuring appropriate plantations within the Sacred Garden
The plantations within the Sacred Garden shall take into account the indigenous species of plants and it will be ensured that the plantations are not mono-cultures.

18   Ensuring protection of river ecosystems around the Sacred Garden

The river ecosystems of the Harhawa and Telar rivers that flow through the Sacred Garden will be protected in respect to water management and pollution right from their sources.

19   *Provisions for an integrated conservation approach for the region*
A regional conservation approach for natural and cultural resources will be established and implemented for the districts of Kapilvastu, Rupendehi and Nawalparasi involving national and international stakeholders.

20   *Ensuring pollution-free environment in and around the Sacred Garden*
Strong measures will be put into place to make the Sacred Garden a pollution-free zone and all polluting activities must be stopped within the Sacred Garden and it must be assured that the external polluting activities do not impact the Sacred Garden.

21   *Provisions for alternative energy sources*
To ensure a pollution free area, alternative energy sources will be prioritized, however ensuring that there is no adverse impact on the property which would also include any visual impact.

Part D. Guidelines to conserve the archaeological vestiges

22   *Safeguarding the testimony to the Birthplace of Lord Buddha*
The protection of the archaeological vestiges that are testimony to Lumbini being the birthplace of Lord Buddha and a site of pilgrimage that spans a period of over two millennia is non-negotiable.

23   *Standardization of the phases of development of Lumbini in antiquity*
The phases of development and linked historic periods are to be standardized to ensure a coherent understanding of the property for purposes of research, interpretation and presentation.

24   *Standardization of the categories of monuments at Lumbini*
The categories of monuments are to be standardized to ensure a coherent understanding of the property for purposes of research, interpretation and presentation.

25   *Activities and interventions to be non-intrusive*
All activities and interventions within the Sacred Garden are to be non-intrusive to the archaeological vestiges.

26   *Activities and interventions to be reversible*
All activities and interventions within the Sacred Garden are to be reversible without causing any damage to the archaeological vestiges and the integrity of the site.

27   *Shelters for archaeological vestiges*
Shelters, whether permanent or temporary, will only be provided for the most significant archaeological vestiges and only if found to be essential for their long-

term conservation and if developed in an appropriate manner.

28 *Archaeological vestiges to remain visible*
The exposed archaeological vestiges are to remain visible to visitors and provisions are to be made for any future archaeological structures to be kept exposed and visible for visitors as long as it does not compromise their long-term conservation.

29 *Clear and truthful interpretation to be provided for visitors*
The archaeological vestiges are to be presented to the visitors in a clear and truthful manner.

30 *Restriction of access onto the archaeological monuments*
Access onto all monuments will be restricted and clearly defined paths and areas will be provided for the visitors and pilgrims.

31 *Provisions for worship and meditation*
Provisions are to be made for worship and mediation which fulfils the requirements of the pilgrims however ensuring the protection of the archaeological vestiges.

32 *Quality and the use of appropriate materials within the Sacred Garden*
Any new construction that takes place within the Sacred Garden will be carried out ensuring good quality and using appropriate materials – with the exception of stone – however these materials must clearly be distinguishable from the archaeological structures.

Part E. Guidelines to provide facilities and services for visitors / pilgrims

33 *Provisions for visitor/pilgrim facilities and services within the Inner Sacred Garden*
Facilities and services shall be provided within the Inner Sacred Garden for the visitor's general requirements that however do not compromise on the sacred atmosphere, harmony, beauty and authenticity of the site and on safeguarding the archaeological vestiges. All such facilities and services must be non-intrusive and reversible.

34 *Removal of inappropriate visitor/pilgrim facilities within the Inner Sacred Garden*
Existing facilities that are inappropriate for the Inner Sacred Garden shall be removed or relocated to a suitable location. All rubble shall be removed from the entire Sacred Garden area. These would be facilities that are not in harmony and not compatible to the natural, historic, religious and archaeological setting.

35 *Provisions for visitor/pilgrim facilities and services within the Outer Sacred Garden*

Facilities and services shall be provided within the Outer Sacred Garden for the visitor's general requirements that however do not compromise on the harmony of the natural setting and ensure a pollution-free environment. Appropriate waste disposal shall be ensured.

36 *Removal of inappropriate visitor facilities within the Outer Sacred Garden*
Existing facilities that are inappropriate for the Outer Sacred Garden shall be removed or relocated to a suitable location. All rubble shall be removed from the entire Sacred Garden. These are the facilities that are contradictory to Kenzo Tange's Master Plan.

37 *Provisions for visitor services outside the Sacred Garden*
Visitor facilities and services where possible will be provided outside the Sacred Garden in keeping with Kenzo Tange's Master Plan.

Part F. Guidelines to regulate activities within the Sacred Garden

38 *Provisions for appropriate activities in the Inner Sacred Garden*
Provisions will be made to allow for appropriate activities in the Inner Sacred Garden nevertheless ensuring the sanctity, harmony and purity of the site. Appropriate activities could be considered those that are very essential for the performance of religious practices, for the preservation and presentation of archaeological vestiges, for the circulation of visitors and pilgrims and for protection and security measures.

39 *Controlling of inappropriate activities within the Inner Sacred Garden*
Provisions will be made to control inappropriate activities in the Inner Sacred Garden to ensure the sanctity, harmony and purity of the site and to safeguard the archaeological vestiges. Inappropriate activities could be considered those that threaten the tranquillity, sanctity and authenticity of the site.

40 *Provisions for appropriate activities in the Outer Sacred Garden*
Provisions will be made to allow for appropriate activities in the Outer Sacred Garden to enhance the experience of the natural environment and to reduce visitor pressure on the Inner Sacred Garden. Appropriate activities could be considered those that are very essential for the performance of religious practices, for the presentation of archaeological vestiges, for the circulation of visitors and for protection and security measures.

41 *Controlling of inappropriate activities within the Outer Sacred Garden*
Provisions will be made to control inappropriate activities in the Outer Sacred Garden to ensure the peace, cleanliness and harmony of the natural environment. Inappropriate activities could be considered those that threaten the tranquillity, sanctity and authenticity of the site.

42 *Balance pilgrim activities and archaeological conservation*

All decisions shall be taken based on the understanding for the need to balance the activities of the pilgrims with the need to conserve and protect the archaeological vestiges of the site.

Part G. Guidelines to control inappropriate development

43   Control inappropriate development within the Sacred Garden
No development work shall be carried out within the entire Sacred Garden other than what is absolutely necessary to conserve the property and provide basic facilities for the visitors/pilgrims, however such activities must be non-intrusive and with a detailed plan for reversibility.

Part H. Guidelines to promote continued research and discourse

44   Developing Lumbini as a Centre for Buddhist Studies
Lumbini shall be promoted as a Centre for Buddhist Studies.

45   Developing Lumbini as the Global Centre for Conservation Ethics
A Global Centre for Conservation Ethics is to be established to expose and help internalise conservation ethics that is needed to heal and care for the earth.

46   Promote research on the archaeological sites in the region
Research on the archaeological sites in the region spanning from Nawalparasi to Kapilbastu districts will be promoted to gain better understanding on the region's ancient history and their linkages to Lumbini.

47   Research on potential archaeological sites in the Sacred Garden
Research on identifying, evaluating and interpreting the physical signature of Lumbini and Associated Sites will be implemented to allow for better presentation, management and long-term protection.

48   Identification of issues and challenges facing archaeological conservation
The long-term issues and challenges facing archaeological conservation must be identified and appropriate responses found based on the most advanced knowledge and technology.

49   Establishment of Consultation processes
Processes shall be put in place to ensure the cooperation and collaboration of all stakeholders in partaking in an appropriate development of the region to ensure the safeguarding of the cultural, natural and spiritual heritage in and around Lumbini.

50   Establishment of Documentation Centre
A documentation centre will be established for all forms of documentation on the cultural and natural heritage of the historic Buddhist Region spanning from Nawalparasi to Kapilbastu.

लुम्बिनी विकास कोषका अध्यक्ष श्री ५ अधिराजकुमार ज्ञानेन्द्र बीर
बिक्रम शाहबाट अन्तर्राष्ट्रिय शान्ति वर्ष १९८६ले शुभ अवसरमा
शान्तिको प्रतीक यो अखण्ड दीप प्रज्वलित गरिबक्सियो । ईति संवत्
२०४३ साल कार्तिक १५गते रोज ७ शुभम् ।

THIS ETERNAL FLAME SYMBOLISING PEACE WAS LIT BY THE
CHAIRMAN OF THE LUMBINI DEVELOPMENT TRUST, HIS ROYAL
HIGHNESS PRINCE GYANENDRA BIR BIKRAM SHAH ON THE
OCCASION OF THE INTERNATIONAL YEAR OF PEACE 1986, ON THE
1st OF NOVEMBER 1986.

Bibliography

Allchen, F.R. and Matsushita, K. 1969. *Report for the Lumbini Development Project.* New York, UNDP.

Allen, C. 2002. *The Buddha and the Sahibs. The Men who Discovered India's Lost Religion.* London, John Murray.

—. 2008. *The Buddha and Dr. Führer. An Archaeological Scandal.* London, Haus Publishing.

Allon, M. 2001. *Three Gāndhārī Ekottarakāgama-Type Sūtras, British Library Kharosthī Fragments 12 and 14* (with a contribution by Andrew Glass). Seattle/London, University of Washington Press. (Gandhāran Buddhist Texts 2.)

Anagarika Dhammapal. 1898. *A Visit to the Lumbini Garden.* Maha Bodhi Journal, Calcutta.

Atzori, A., Cüppers, C., Ghimire, H.L., Rai, R., Suwal, R., Ukesh, B. and Weise, K. 2006. *Lumbini. Present Status and Future Challenges.* Kathmandu, UNESCO. http://unesdoc.unesco.org/images/0014/001471/147105e.pdf (Accessed 2 October 2013.)

Bareau, A. 1974. La Jeunesse du Buddha dans les Sūtrapitaka et les Vinayapitakaanciens. *Bulletin de l'École Française d'Extrême Orient, Tome* 61, pp. 199–274.

—. 1995. Lumbinī et la Naissance du Futur Buddha. *Recherches sur la biographie du Buddha dans les Sūtrapitaka et les Vinayapitaka anciens III.* Articles complémentaires. Paris, École Française d'Extrême Orient, pp. 1-13 (Monographie / École française d'Extrême-Orient, 178.)

Bechert, H. (ed.). 1991, 1992. *The Dating of the Historical Buddha / Die Datierung des Historischen Buddha, Part 1 & 2.*Göttingen, Vandenhoeck &Ruprecht (Symposien zur Buddhismusforschung, IV, 1 & 2). (Abhandlungen der Akademie der Wissenschaften in Göttingen, 189 & 194.)

Beal, S. 1983. *Si-Yu-Kior the Buddhist Records of the Western World, Munshiram Manoharlal, Translated from the Chinese of HiuenTsiang AD 629.* New Delhi, India MunshiramManoharlal Publishers.

—. 1993. *Travels of Fa-hien and Sung-yun, Buddhist Pilgrims from China to India, (400-518 A.D.).* New Delhi. Asian Educational Services

Bidari, B. 2000. The Nativity Tree of Prince Siddhartha. *The Maha-Bodhi: The Journal of the Maha Bodhi Society of India.* Calcutta, Maha Bodhi Society, pp. 18-29.

—. 2004. *Lumbini: A Haven of Sacred Refuge.* Kathmandu, Third Impression.

—. 2009. *Lumbini Beckons. A Glimpse of the Holy Birthplace of the Buddha and its Master Plan and the Ashoka Pillar Inscription and the Marker Stone 'The exact birth spot of the Buddha'.* Lumbini.

Boccardi, G. and Gupta, D. 2005. *UNESCO- ICOMOS Joint Mission to Lumbini, World Heritage Site – November 2005. Mission Report. Reactive Monitoring Mission to Lumbini, the Birthplace of the Lord Buddha, World Heritage Property, Nepal (13-18th Nov, 2005).* Paris, UNESCO. http://whc.unesco.org/archive/2006/mis666-2005.pdf (Accessed 2 October 2013.)

Buddha Dharma Education Association Inc. 2008. Buddhism in South Asia, India, Srilanka. http://www.buddhanet.net/e-learning/buddhistworld/south-asia.htm (Accessed 4 February 2013.)

Coningham, R.A.E. 2001.The Archaeology of Buddhism. T. Insoll (ed.) *Archaeology and World Religion.* London, Routledge, pp. 61-91.

—. 2009. Identifying, Evaluating and Interpreting the Physical Signature of Lumbini and Associated Sites for Presentation, Management and long-term Protection. Report, UNESCO, Kathmandu, p. 15.

Coningham, R.A.E., and Milou, J.F. 2000. Reactive Monitoring Mission to Lumbini, Birthplace of Lord Buddha. Report, UNESCO, Kathmandu.

Coningham, R.A.E., Schmidt, A.R. and Strickland, K.M. 2011. A Pilot Geophysical and Auger Core Evaluation within the UNESCO World Heritage Site of Lumbini, Nepal. *Ancient Nepal,* No. 176, pp. 9-24.

—. 2002. Geophysical, Auger, Environmental and Visitor Survey of the Core Zone of the Lumbini World Heritage Site, Nepal. Report, UNESCO, Kathmandu.

Cueppers, C., Deeg, M. and Durt, H. (eds). 2010. *The Birth of the Buddha. Proceedings of the Seminar held in Lumbini, Nepal, October 2004.* Lumbini, Lumbini International Research Institute. (LIRI Seminar Proceedings Series, Vol. 3.)

Davids, T.W.R. 1880. *Buddhist Birth-Stories or Jāntaka Tales.* London, Trübner and Co. (Reprint Winsome Books India, 2004), pp. 153-155.

Deeg, M. 2003. *The Places where Siddhārtha Trod: Lumbinī and Kapilavastu.* Lumbini, Lumbinī International Research Institute.

—. 2005. *Das Gaoseng-Faxian-Zhuan als religionsgeschichtliche Quelle. Der älteste Bericht eines chinesischen buddhistischen Pilgermönchs über seine Reise nach Indien mit Übersetzung des Textes.* Studies in Oriental Religions, Vol. 52, Harrassowitz Verlag.

Deo, S.B. 1968. *Archaeological Investigations in the Nepal Terai: 1964.* Kathmandu, Department of Archaeology.

Derrett, J.D.M. 1995. *Two Masters: The Buddha and Jesus.* Northamptonshire,

Pilkington Press.

—. 2000. *The Bible and the Buddhists.* Bornato in Franciacorta, Casa Editrice Sardini. (Supplementum di Bibbia e oriente, 11.)

Erdosy, G. 1995. F.R. Allchin (ed.), The Prelude to Urbanization: Ethnicity and the Rise of the Late Vedic Chiefdoms. *The Archaeology of Early Historic South Asia.* Cambridge, Cambridge University Press, pp. 75-99.

Falk, H. 1998. *The Discovery of Lumbini.* Lumbini, Lumbini International Research Institute (Lumbini International Research Institute Occasional Papers, 1) (original German version in: Acta Orientalia 52 (1991), pp. 70-90).

Foster, B. & M. 1998. *The Secret Lives of Alexandra David-Neel.* Woodstock, Overlook Press.

Foucaux, P.E. 1847-1848. *Rgyatch'errolpa ou Développement des Jeux contenant l'histoire du Bouddha Çakya-Mouni.* Paris, L'Imprimerie royale.

Foucher, A. 1949. *La vie du Bouddha d'après les textes et les monuments de l'Inde.* Paris, Payot (quoted after the reprint 1987. Paris, Jean Maisonneuve) (first Indian edition 2003, translated by Simone Brangier Boas.)

Führer, A. 1972. *Antiquities of Buddha Sakyamuni's Birthplace in the Nepalese Tarai.* Varanasi, Indological Book House. (Archaeological Survey of Northern India, Vol. 6, New imperial series, Archaeological Survey of India, Vol. 26, New imperial series / Northern India, New imperial series, Archaeological Survey of India, 1889, Vol. 6.)

Fukita, T. 2003. *The Mahāvadānasūtra. A New Edition Based on Manuscripts Discovered in Northern Turkestan.* Göttingen, Vandenhoeck & Rupprecht (Sanskrit-Wörterbuch der buddhistischen Texte aus den Turfan-Funden, Beiheft 10.)

Garbe, R. 1914. *Indien und das Christentum. Eine Untersuchung der religionsgeschichtlichen Zusammenhänge.* Tübingen, Mohr.

Glass, A. 2007. Four *Gāndhārī Samyuktāgama Sūtras: Senior Kharosthī Fragment 5.* Seattle, University of Washington Press. (Gandhāran Buddhist Texts 4.)

Government of Nepal. 1996. World Heritage Committee Nomination Document for Lumbini, the Birthplace of the Lord Buddha, archaeological conservation area. Nomination Document, GoN, Nepal.

Grönbold, G. 1985. *Jesus in Indien. Das Ende einer Legende.* München, Kösel.

Gyatso, N.K.L., Stearns, C. and Stearns, M. 1986. *Fortunate to Behold: An Explanation of the Nativity of Śākyamuni Buddha at Lumbini Garden, together with an Historical Account of Kapilavastu and Devadaha, and Some Additional Discourses.* Kathmandu, Gyatso, N.K.L., Stearns, C. and Stearns, M.

Härtel, H. 1991. Archaeological Research on Ancient Buddhist Sites. Bechert, pp. 61-89.

Harvey, P. 2000. *An Introduction to Buddhist Ethics: Foundations, Values, and Issues.* Cambridge, Cambridge University Press.

—. 2004. *An Introduction to Buddhism, Teaching, History and Practices,* Cambridge, Cambridge University Press. South Asian Edition Reprint 2005.

Hinüber, O. V. 1986. *Das ältere Mittelindisch im Überblick.* Wien, Verlag der Österreichischen Akademie der Wissenschaften.

—. 1989. *Der Beginn der Schrift und frühe Schriftlichkeit in Indien,* Wiesbaden, Akademie der Wissenschaften und der Literatur (Abhandlungen der Geistes- und sozialwissenschaftlichen Klasse, Jg. 1989, Nr. 11) (Göttingische Gelehrte Anzeigen Jg. 246, H. 3/4 (1994), 207-224.)

—. 1997. *A Handbook of Pali Literature.* Berlin, New York, Walter de Gruyter (Indian philology and South Asian studies, Vol. 2.)

—. 2001: *Das ältere Mittel indisch im Überblick.* Vienna, Verlag der Österreichischen Akademie der Wissenschaften. (Veröffentlichungen der Kommission für Sprachen und Kulturen Südasiens, Heft 20) (Sitzungsberichte (Österreichische Akademie der Wissenschaften., Philosophisch-Historische Klasse) Bd. 467).)

ICOMOS. 1996. World Heritage List, Lumbini (Nepal), No.C666 rev. ICOMOS Recommendations on the Inscription of Lumbini on the List of World Heritage, September, 1996 http://whc.unesco.org/archive/advisory_body_evaluation/666rev.pdf (Access 2 October 2013).

World Heritage Committee. 1993. *Report of the seventeenth session of the World Heritage Committee in Cartagena, Colombia,* Paris, UNESCO (Doc. WHC-93/CONF.002/14).

Japan Buddhist Federation. 2001. *Archaeological Research at Mayadevi Temple, Lumbini.* Tokyo, Japan Buddhist Federation.

—. 2005. *Lumbini: The Archaeological Survey Report 1992- 1995.* Tokyo, Japan Buddhist Federation.

Johnston, E.H. 1972. *Buddhacarita or Acts of the Buddha. Cantos I to xiv.* Delhi, Motilal Banarsidass.

Khosla, S. 1991. *Lalitavistara and the Evolution of the Buddha Legend.* Delhi, Galaxy Publications.

Kohn, L. 1998. *God of the Dao. Lord Lao in History and Myth.* Ann Arbor, MI, The University of Michigan Press.

DeKörös, C.A. 1991. *Notices on the Life of Sakya. Extracted from the Tibetan Authorities.* New Delhi, Tibetan Studies, pp. 231-317 (Original 1839.)

Lannoy, R. 1971. *The Speaking Tree: A Study of Indian Culture and Society.* Oxford, Oxford University Press.

Lenz, T. 2002. *A New Version of the GāndhārīDharmapada and a Collection of Previous-Birth Stories. British Library Kharosthī Fragments 16 + 25.* Seattle, London: University of Washington Press. (Gandhāran Buddhist texts, Vol. 3.)

Leoshko, J. 2003. *Sacred Traces: British Exploration of Buddhism in India.* Hants, Ashgate.

Lillie, A. 1883.*The Popular Life of Buddha, containing an answer to the 'Hibert Lectures' of 1881.* London, K. Paul, Trench &Co. (Reprint 2005. Delhi, Winsome Books), pp. 9-10.

Lopez, D.S. 2005. *Critical Terms for the Study of Buddhism.* Chicago, University of Chicago Press.

Lüders, H. 1911. *BruchstückebuddhistischerDramen.* Berlin, Georg Reimer (Kleinere Sanskrit-Texte, Heft 1).

Luczanits, C. 1993. *The Sources for Bu-ston's Introduction to the Acts of a Buddha.* Wiener Zeitschrift für die Kunde Südasiens, Vol. 37, pp. 93-108.

Lumbini Development Trust. 2011. Retrospective Statement of Outstanding Universal Value. Submitted to the World Heritage Centre on 1 February 2011. LDT, Nepal.

—. 2013. Integrated Management Framework Document. Proposed framework for the management of Lumbini, GoN, Nepal.

Lumbini Institutions. 2006. A Buddhist Vision for the Sacred Garden. Prepared by the Lumbini Institutions, Lumbini Garden on 21 April 2006.

Maha-parinibbanaSutta: Last Days of the Buddha (DN 16), translated from the Pali by Sister Vajira & Francis Story.http://www.accesstoinsight.org/tipitaka/dn/dn.16.1-6.vaji.html (Accessed 2 October 2013).

Malalasekera, G. P. 1983. *Dictionary of Pali Proper Names.* London, Published for the Pali Text Society by Luzac & Co. (Originally published in 1937.)

Meucci, C. 2012. Strengthening the Conservation and Management of Lumbini, the birthplace of the Lord Buddha. Conservation Activity. UNESCO, Kathmandu.

Michaels, A. and Ulrich, L. 2002. *Jesus und Buddha. Leben und Lehre im Vergleich.* München,Verlag C.H Beck (English Translation: 2006. Encountering Jesus & Buddha: Their Lives and Teachings. Minneapolis, Fortress Press.)

Mishra, T. N. 1996. The Archaeological Activities in Lumbini. *Ancient Nepal,* No. 13, pp. 36-48.

Mitra, D. 1971. *Buddhist Monuments.* Calcutta, Sahitya Samsad.

—. 1972. Excavations at Tilaura-Kot and Kodan and the Explorations in the Nepalese Tarai. Kathmandu, Department of Archaeology.

Mukherji, P.C. 1969. *A Report on a Tour of Exploration of the Antiquities of Kapilavastu Tarai of Nepal during February and March 1899*. Delhi, Indological Book House.

Nhất Hạnh, T. 2008. *The World We Have: A Buddhist Approach to Peace and Ecology*. Berkeley, Parallax Press.

Nanamoli, B. 1972. *The Life of the Buddha as it appears in the Pali Canon, the oldest authentic record*. Kandy, Buddhist Publication Society.

Norman, K.R. (transl.). 1996. *The Rhinoceros Horn and other Early Buddhist Poems (Sutta-NipAta)*. London [u.a.], Pali Text Society.

O'Brien, B. Buddhist Scriptures: An Overview. http://buddhism.about.com/od/sacredbuddhisttexts/a/buddhist-scriptures.htm (Accessed 2 October 2013.)

Petech, L. 1950. *Northern India According to the Shui-ching-chu*. Roma,Is. M. E. O. (Serie orientale Roma, Vol. 2.)

Pischel, R. 1917. *Leben und Lehre des Buddha. Durchgesehen von Heinrich Lüders. Leipzig*, Berlin, B.G. Teubner (quoted after the reprint 1982 Wiesbaden, Franz Steiner Verlag. (Kölner Sarasvati Series 4.)

Pradhan, B.L. 1979. *Lumbini-Kapilavastu-Devadaha*.Kathmandu, Research Center for Nepal & Asian Studies.

Przyluski, J. 1967. The Legend of Emperor Aśoka in Indian and Chinese Texts. Calcutta, Firma K.L.Mukhopadhyaya, pp. 29-30.

Rana, D. 1999. *The Role of General Khadga Shumsher Rana in the Discovery of Lumbini*. Lumbini, International Buddhist Society, Annual Publication 5, pp. 12-14.

Reynolds, F. 1976. The Many Lives of Buddha. A Study of Sacred Biography and Theravāda Tradition. F. Reynolds and D. Capps (eds). *The Biographical Process. Studies in the History and Psychology of Religion*.The Hague, Mouton, pp. 37-61. (Religion and reason, 11.)

—. 1997. Rebirth Traditions and the Lineages of Gotama: A Study in Theravāda Buddhology. J. Schober (ed.). *Sacred Biography in the Buddhist Tradition of South and Southeast Asia*. Honolulu, University of Hawai'i Press, pp. 19-39.

Rijal, K. 1979. *Archaeological Remains of Kapilavastu, Lumbini, and Devadaha*. Kathmandu, Educational Enterprises.

—. 1996. *100 Years of Archaeological Research in Lumbini, Kapilavastu, Devadaha*. Kathmandu, S.K. International Publishing House.

Rockhill, W.W. 1991. *The Life of the Buddha and the Early History of His Order*. New Delhi, Navrang. (First edition London, Kegan Paul, Trench, Trübner & Co., 1892.)

Saint-Hilaire, J. B. 1952. *Hiouen-Thsang in India*. Calcutta, Anil Gupta.(Reprint 2003.

New Delhi, Rupa.)

Salomon, R. 1999. *Ancient Buddhist Scrolls form Gandhāra. The British Library Kharosthī Fragments.* Seattle, University of Washington Press.

—. 2000. *A Gāndhārī version of the Rhinoceros Sūtra. British Library Kharoṣṭhī fragment 5B.*Seattle, University of Washington Press.(Gandhāran Buddhist texts, Vol.1.)

Samdhong, R. 1987. *Ten Suttas from "Dīgha Nikāya" : Long discourses of the Buddha.* Sarnath, Varanasi, Central Institute of Higher Tibetan Studies. (Bibliotheca Indo-Tibetica, 12.)

Schmithausen, L. 1990. *Buddhism and Nature.* In: Proceedings of an International Symposium on the Occasion of EXPO 1990. Tokyo, The International Institute for Buddhist Studies, 1991, pp. 22-35. (Studia philologica Buddhic, Occasional paper series, 7).

Schneider, U. 1982. *Einführung in den Buddhismus.* Darmstadt, Wissenschaftliche Buchgesellschaft.

Schumann, W. 1989. *The Historical Buddha: The Times, Lives and Teachings of the Founder of Buddhism.* London, Arkana (English translation of the German original: 1982 *Der historische Buddha. Leben und Lehre des Gotama.* Köln, Diederichs).

Second World Buddhist Summit, 2004. Declaration. http://www.bdcu.org.au/bddronline/bddr15no1/LumbiniSummitReport.pdf (Accessed 2 October 2013.)

Saxe, J. G., *The Blind Men and the Elephant.* http://www.co-intelligence.org/blindmenelephant.html (Accessed 2 October 2013.)

Sircar, D.C. 1967. *Inscriptions of Asoka.* New Delhi, Publications Division, Ministry of Information and Broadcasting, Govt. of India.

Smith, V.A. 1897. The Birthplace of Gautama Buddha. *Journal of the Royal Asiatic Society of Great Britain and Ireland,* pp. 615-621.

Stovel, H. 2008. Conserving the sacred: special challenges for World Heritage Sites. *World Heritage Review,* No. 51, pp. 26-33. Paris, UNESCO.

Strauch, I. 2007. *The Bajaur collection: A new collection of Kharoecti manuscripts. A preliminary catalogue and survey.* http://www.geschkult.fu-berlin.de/e/indologie/bajaur/publication/index.html (Accessed 19 October 2013).

Strong, J. 2001. The Buddha. A Short Biography. Oxford, Oneworld.

Subedi, A. 1999.*Ekai Kawaguchi: The Trespassing Insider.* Kathmandu, Mandala Book Point.

Tange, K. and Urtec. 1972. Final Outline Design for Lumbini. Report, New York,

United Nations.

—. 1976. Master Design for the Development of Lumbini, Phase II, Stage I. Report, New York, United Nations.

—. 1977. Master Design for the Development of Lumbini, Phase II, Stage II. Report, New York, United Nations.

—. 1978. Master Design for the Development of Lumbini, Phase II. Final Report, New York, United Nations.

—. 1979. Architectural Design for the Lumbini Garden Phase III, Stage I. Report, New York, United Nations.

—. 1981. Architectural Design for the Lumbini Garden Phase III, Stage II. Report, New York, United Nations.

Tange, K. 1980. *Kenzo Tange*. SD Edition Department, Kashima Publication.

Thomas, E.J. 1949. *The Life of the Buddha as Legend and History.* 3rd edition. London, Routledge and Kegan Paul Ltd.

Thundy, Z.P. 1993. *Buddha and Christ. Nativity Stories and Indian Traditions.* Leiden, New York, E.J. Brill. (Studies in the History of Religions, 60).

Translating the Words of the Buddha. The play in full. http://read.84000. co/#!ReadingRoom/UT22084-046-001/82 (Accessed 4 February 2013.)

Tucci, G. 1977. *Journey to Mustang,* 1952. Kathmandu, Ratna Pustak Bhandar. (Bibliotheca Himalayica, Series 1, Vol. 23.)

UNESCO. 2013. *Lumbini, The birthplace of Lord Buddha in Nepal, Completing the Kenzo Tange Master Plan.* Kathmandu, UNESCO.

United Nations. 1970. *Brochure on Lumbini, The Birthplace of Buddha.* New York, International Committee for the Development of Lumbini.

—. 1971. Report of the Advisory Panel International Committee for the Development of Lumbini (ICDL). New York, United Nations.

Waddell, L.A., Wylie, H. and Konstam, E.H. 1897. The Discovery of the Birthplace of the Buddha. *Journal of the Royal Asiatic Society of Great Britain and Ireland,* pp. 644-651.

Waldschmidt, E. 1944, 1948. *Die Überlieferung vom Lebensende des Buddha. Eine vergleichende Analyse des Mahāparinirvānasūtra und seiner Textentsprechungen.* Göttingen, Vandenhoeck& Ruprecht.(Akademie der Wissenschaften in Göttingen;Philologisch-Historische Klasse; Abhandlungen 29 + 30).

—. 1950, 1951. *Das Mahāparinirvānasūtra. Text in Sanskrit und Tibetisch, verglichen mit dem Pāli nebst einer Übersetzung der chinesischen Entsprechung im Vinaya der Mūlasarvāstivādins.* 3 parts. Berlin: Adademie Verlag (Abhandlungen der

Akademie der Wissenschaften Berlin, Klasse für Sprachen, Literatur und Kunst Jg. 1949, no.1, Jg. 1950, no.2, Jg. 1950, no.3).

—. 1953, 1956. *Das Mahāvadānasūtra, ein kanonischer Text über die sieben letz-ten Buddhas. Sanskrit, verglichen mit dem Pāli nebst einer Analyse der in chinesi-scher Übersetzung überlieferten Parallelversionen,* 2 parts. Berlin: Adademie Verlag (Abhandlungen der Deutschen Akademie der Wissenschaften zu Berlin, Klasse für Sprachen, Literatur und Kunst, Jg. 1952, no.8, and Jg. 1954 no.3).

Walsch, M. 1998. *Digha Nikya: The Long Discourse of the Buddha.* Boston, Wisdom Publication.

Watters, T. 1973. *On Yuan Chwang's Travels in India.* New Delhi, Munshiram Manoharlal.

Weise, K. and Shrestha, M. 2008. Defining the World Heritage Site — Identification of 'the place to be managed'. Report. UNESCO, Kathmandu.

Weise, K. 1992. Der Wald im Hinduistischen Kontext. Ein Bild meiner Vorstellungen. Thesis, Swiss Federal Institute of Technology, Switzerland.

—. 2008. Lumbini the birthplace of Lord Buddha, World Heritage Site, Integrated Management Plan, Plan of Actions and Management Frameworks. Kathmandu, Report, UNESCO, Kathmandu.

Windisch, Ernst. 1908. *Buddhas Geburt und die Lehre von der Seelenwanderung.* Leipzig: B.G. Teubner (Abhandlungen der Philologisch-Historischen Klasse der Königl. SächsischenGesellschaft der Wissenschaften, 26. Bd., No. 2).

Woodward, M.R. 1997. The Biographical Imperative in Theravāda Buddhism. J. Schober (ed.). *Sacred Biography in the Buddhist Tradition of South and Southeast Asia.* Honolulu, University of Hawai'i Press, pp. 40-63.

World Heritage Committee. 1993. Report of the seventeenth session of the World Heritage Committee in Cartagena, Colombia. Paris, UNESCO. (Doc. WHC-93/CONF.002/14.)

World Heritage Committee. 1997. Report of the twenty-first session of the World Heritage Committee, Naples, Italy. http://whc.unesco.org/archive/repcom97.htm#666 (Doc. WHC-97/CONF.208/17.)

World Heritage Committee, 2011. State of conservation of World Heritage properties inscribed on the World Heritage List. Paris, UNESCO. (Doc. WHC-11/35.COM/7B.)

World Heritage Committee, 2012. State of conservation of World Heritage properties inscribed on the World Heritage List. Paris, UNESCO. (Doc. WHC-12/36.COM/7B.)

Abbreviations

BCE	Before the Common Era
CE	Christian Era
DFID	Department for International Development
DoA	Department of Archaeology
EIA	Environmental Impact Assessment
EPA	Environment Protection Act
GoN	Government of Nepal
ICDL	International Committee for the Development of Lumbini
ICOMOS	International Council on Monuments and Sites
IMP	Integrated Management Plan
IUCN	International Union for Conservation of Nature
JBF	Japanese Buddhist Federation
JFIT	Japanese Funds-in-Trust
LCCC	Lumbini Crane Conservation Centre
LDT	Lumbini Development Trust
LPZ	Lumbini Protected Zone
NBP	Northern Black Polished ware
NGO	Non-Governmental Organization
OUV	Outstanding Universal Value
SNV	Netherlands Development Organization
TU	Tribhuvan University
UN	United Nations
UNDP	United Nations Development Programme
UNESCO	United Nations Educational, Scientific and Cultural Organization
WH	World Heritage